The Financial Pocketknife challenged me to think about investment differently and reconcile the false belief that the only way to become wealthy was to play the stock market and get lucky day trading.

Seth Meisel – Denver, CO

I was expecting to be bored reading about financial stuff but knew I needed to learn about personal finance. To my pleasant surprise, the book was actually fun to read. The author found a way to explain things easily while showing some personality!

Kristy Peacock – Seminole, FL

I was amazed to learn how many benefits IUL offers. I never knew life insurance did so much more than just pay a death benefit when you died. I was surprised to learn about the investment options and tax savings.

Tim Arrington - Canton, GA

This is an excellent book, with both professional and personal insights to help educate the general public.

Steve Jecker – Prospect, KY

I didn't know what I didn't know! That there was financial tool that could do so many things.

Ryan Cushman – Cumming, GA

Dedicated to the millions of overlooked families who have a need for financial education!

With great appreciation to:

Laura, my best friend and soul mate.

Mom, the most resilient and hardworking person I know.

Jim and Sandy Scott, awesome life models.

Erik Bigalke, my loyal heavy metal brother.

Lisa Pelamati Creswell, a great friend. You are missed.

"Financial Pocketknife®" is a metaphoric term used to conceptually describe the features and benefits of Indexed Universal Life Insurance; however, it is not an actual product or a specific strategy. The purpose of the Financial Pocketknife analogy is to act as a tool in educating the public on a complicated financial concept. Before making any decisions on the suitability of such a product for your personal circumstances, you should consult a financial advisor and other professionals, including but not limited to, your tax and legal professionals.

Table of Contents

Pregame

Begin with the end in mind.

Stephen Covey

SHHHH! It's a secret. Not for those in the "affluent" market but somehow it is for the rest of us. The early generation of it was a financial product that has been used by Walt Disney to create his majestic empire, by Ray Kroc to change the world's dining habits with McDonald's, and by Jacques Penney to fund his historic retail juggernaut.

- From its infancy in 2006 through 2016, it has grown from 3% of industry sales to 21%!
- While the affluent comprise only about 10 % of the population, they account for almost half of the market utilization. (Federal Reserve)
- As wealth increases, so does its ownership. While 16.7% of non-affluent households own it, up to 40.5% of affluent households own it.

(Federal Reserve: Non-affluent equals less than $250,000 in assets)

Despite such powerful benefits and rising popularity, the vast majority of people still don't know about it. Yet, it is available and readily accessible to anyone who qualifies for it. It shouldn't be a secret at all, but why is it?

The root cause for this lack of awareness is that its features can be complicated. Most financial professionals don't understand it. The financial gurus on TV definitely don't comprehend it. Those who learn about it question if it is too good to be true. And for those few professionals who do understand it, they have a difficult time explaining it and are trained to hunt "big game" in the affluent market.

Now, there is nothing wrong with being affluent. In fact, we should applaud personal success. Certainly, most of us strive to become secure, wealthy and contribute to meaningful causes. But what about the "Average Joe and Josephine"? If they desire these same opportunities, doesn't it make sense that they use the same resources and tools that the wealthy use? Shouldn't they have the same opportunity to learn about powerful financial concepts and access to professional help?

Believe it or not, I once had a snobby life insurance attorney who said, "This product (The Financial Pocketknife®) isn't really good for the middle class because it is very complicated." I translated his statement to mean: "Middle class people are too stupid to understand the product, and therefore, should not own it." I responded by asking if he could tell me how his smart phone application worked. When he said, "No, I'm an attorney, not a programmer," I asked if he really deserves to own a smart phone. After all, if he doesn't understand how it works, by his own reasoning he shouldn't be able to enjoy its many benefits.

The point is that one doesn't have to understand computer programming to understand the great benefits of a smart phone. And, one doesn't need to understand the actuarial science of a financial product to understand its benefits. By the way, I guarantee you that the technical aspect of the product is equally difficult for everyone, including the attorney.

The good news is that this book was written to help everyone, regardless of wealth status or educational level, understand how the Financial Pocketknife works and the many benefits it provides (even our arrogant life insurance attorney). I do believe, however, that middle class families need this product more than any other demographic group. After all, they are the ones most vulnerable to financial challenges in this modern economy of technology and globalization.

Statistics show that the gap between the wealthy and poor in the United States is consistently widening as the middle class continues to experience increasing financial pressures. I'm a strong believer that those in the middle class are at a crossroads in time where they will either struggle financially for years to come or prosper in the new economy based on the financial and career decisions they make today. No longer will people be able to join a company, work for 40 years, and retire with a company pension plan. Rather, they will have to become more self-reliant, entrepreneurial and financially astute.

Make no mistake about it, our country is in substantial financial distress despite what any politician tells you or how little attention the media gives it. From a macro level (U.S. economy), real wages have been stagnant for decades, the division between the classes has grown precipitously, and the national debt has reached $21,500,000,000,000 ($21.5 trillion) or $61,000 per citizen. That's $240,000 per family of four. If we study history, we see that dominant civilizations implode, and revolutions occur when economies collapse.

Yet, we don't flinch about this as we go about our daily lives – in part, because our society doesn't understand economics, but primarily because we are focused on our own financial and life challenges.

Despite the fact there has never been a more prosperous country in the history of the world, most Americans are struggling and facing great financial challenges. Let's look at the staggering financial challenges that Americans face and related statistics.

Median U.S. household income is $59,036 (Department of Labor, 2016), yet:
- Debt is high
    - Consumer debt = $13 trillion (Fed)
    - Household credit card debt = $8,377 (Wallethub)
    - Average consumer has 13 credit obligations (myfico.com)
    - $51 billion in fast food on debit and credit cards (carddata.com)
    - More than 1 billion VISA cards worldwide, 450 million in U.S.
    - Average credit card rate = 16.47% (creditcard.com)
    - 4 credit cards per consumer (Experian)
    - Bankruptcy filings = 1,137,978 (uscourts.gov, 2016)

- Savings are low
    - U.S. savings rate = 2.4% in 2016 vs. 11.1% in 1985 (Fed)
    - 53% of workers have less than $25,000 savings (*USA Today*)
    - 50% of families could only last 4-6 months on their savings
    - 26 % of people ages 50-54 and 14% of those age 65 and older have no savings
    - 1/3 of those ages 30-49 have yet to start putting something away for their later years

- The median retirement account balance for all working-age households in the U.S. is $3,000, and $12,000 for near-retirement households (National Institute on Retirement Security)
- International Savings Rate
  - Europe =20%, Japan = 25%, China = 50%

- Americans are living longer and need more money
  - In 1900, the average lifespan was 47, but now it's 78
  - An American can spend 20-30 years in retirement

- Retirement responsibility has been shifted from companies to individuals
  - Since 1985, 80,000 of 112,000 pension plans have been terminated
  - Social Security: Benefits begin later than the original age of 65 and long-term solvency issues are questionable

- Financial struggles impact relationships
  - U.S. leads the West in divorce rate (up to 50%)
  - Financial pressures are a leading cause of divorce

- Belief in the "American Dream" is dwindling
  - Seven in 10 believe it is getting harder and harder to live a middle-class lifestyle, and only about half feel the "American Dream" is still alive (LIMRA)
  - Seven in 10 married households with children under age 18 would only be able to meet everyday living expenses for a few months if a primary wage earner died

These statistics paint a dismal picture for the average family and highlight the importance of financial education and professional help. Yet, most financial professionals and companies ignore the average family. Their herd mentality and monolithic thinking lead them to seek out larger affluent clients. They believe that the middle-class market segments are not profitable and are best served by visiting a company's website for self-service.

Meanwhile, ignored Americans inspiring to become financially independent are in need and want help.

- Investors who have professional help average 2.93% greater return than those without, net of fees. (AON/Hewitt)

- More than 1 in 4 Americans say they do not have enough life insurance protection. This number jumps to 40 % when looking at consumers making less than $50,000 per year.

- 28% cite that they have not secured life insurance because no one has approached them about it. (LIMRA, 2016)

- The middle-class market has a $1.4 billion annual premium gap in which consumers need and desire financial guidance but are being ignored by the industry.

- Nearly 1/4 of households with children under the age of 18 want to speak to an agent but will not proactively seek one.

Although these insights may seem bleak, there is hope. In fact, there is great hope and opportunity for those who learn how the money game is played and take responsibility for their own financial success and dreams.

My mission in writing this book is to help you with this meaningful endeavor. I believe that ALL families should be educated on financial concepts and exposed to the powerful tools that exist to help them thrive in today's modern economy.

It's a Calling

Not all of us figure it out, but we all have a calling and purpose for our life. For some, it may be spiritual. For others, it may be to serve in the medical field or become a musician or artist. But for most, it may have less glamour or public recognition. For me, it is to educate "everyday" people on financial matters. You see, I am "everyday" people. I come from a humble background, raised by a single mom (the most difficult job in the world). Maybe it was because of our family's constant financial struggles growing up that I wanted to learn everything I could about financial issues.

Yet, even after graduating high school, obtaining a B.S. in Finance, and an MBA, I never once had a class focused on the subject of personal finance. I studied obscure subjects such as Astronomy, French, Revitalizing Cities, Russian Politics and Voltaire but never learned about buying a car, securing a mortgage, investing in mutual funds or obtaining life insurance – all financial issues that every one of us needs to understand. Ironically, the most important things that we need to learn to become financially secure in life are not taught to us in school.

This statement is not an indictment of educators but rather on our culture as a whole. Our society, in general, doesn't feel financial literacy is important. How else can one explain that there are only four states that require students to complete a personal finance class to graduate from high school? Yet, it may be the most important subject one can ever learn and something that affects everyone. The use of financial concepts WILL be used in real life and can determine the quality of life we live, as well as that of our children and grandchildren.

In the chapters to come, I will share with you financial, practical, and psychological insights I have learned during more than 25 years in the financial services field. I have been fortunate enough to work with thousands of people in many different capacities. I've worked hand-in-hand with billion-dollar money managers, life insurance CEOs, mailroom employees, compliance specialists, actuaries, attorneys, accountants, academics, transaction processors, marketing organizations, financial planners, customer service reps, product developers, IT managers, wholesalers, college students and most importantly, my own clients.

This vast experience has enabled me to not only become an expert in the field but also to understand the industry from every imaginable perspective. I understand the different thought processes that exist in financial services, the theories on how to invest and mitigate risk, and the marketing messages that are prevalent based on biased motives.

I share this background with you not to sound self-promoting or boastful, but to share with you that with all the experience I have acquired and knowledge I have gained over the years, The Financial Pocketknife® is the best foundational tool to serve families that I have ever come across.

The Financial Pocketknife® is not suitable for everyone…. but let me state unequivocally, 100%, without a doubt, it is one of the most powerful financial tools ever designed to help families build a strong financial foundation.

And while The Financial Pocketknife may or may not be a good strategy for you individually, without question it is one that you should know about and consider if it meets your needs.

If you don't believe me, I have an opportunity for you at the end of the book that you can use to challenge my statement. (Don't ruin it by going there now.)

As the term implies, "financial foundation" is not all-encompassing. It refers to the basics. I'm a big fan of basics. I believe that football games are won by blocking and tackling, that A's are earned by studying at the library, that great guitar players know the 12-bar blues, and that you win the financial game by saving wisely and protecting your assets. Of course, we typically desire more than a foundation and may need other tools and techniques to reach our goals, but all the glitzy stuff doesn't happen without a strong foundation.

While each individual is unique based on goals, time horizon and circumstances, there are some qualifiers for people who may benefit from The Financial Pocketknife®:

- ☐ You have personal dreams and goals that you have yet to achieve.
- ☐ You cannot predict your future with 100% certainty.
- ☐ You need flexibility in your strategy to adjust to life events.
- ☐ You have (or will have) others who depend on you financially.
- ☐ You have a need to develop a long-term financial strategy.
- ☐ You have a desire to maximize your savings returns but are concerned about market risk.
- ☐ You prefer not to pay more taxes than you are legally required.
- ☐ You are relatively healthy.
- ☐ You desire convenience.

Challenges

There are three big challenges I experience when discussing financial issues with people. First, most people find the subject of personal finance to be very boring, as my wife reminds me on a regular basis. Second, financial topics can be very complicated no matter who you are, your education level or life experience. Third, managing financial matters is time consuming and can require a lot of work to manage.

When people think of personal finance, they typically associate it with budgeting, financial strategies, taxes, the stock market and a myriad of other technical topics. While there are many finance nerds like myself who love this type of stuff and get excited about such topics, most people avoid the subject like the plague. They would rather have a dentist drill for cavities than deal with financial issues. As you will notice throughout the book, I don't believe learning about financial issues and having fun need to be mutually exclusive events. I have taken great effort to deliver important information in such a way that you won't want to jump off a bridge while reading – although it may take you some time to pick up on my bad "dad jokes" and sarcasm.

Sadly, many people are never exposed to the benefits of "The Financial Pocketknife®" because it is thought to be too complex for the Average Joe and yet these are the people who may benefit the most from its features. I don't have to know how my car works to drive it or how my computer works to use it. But I do know "how" they benefit me and the value they provide to my everyday life. Likewise, one doesn't have to understand the actuarial algorithms, cite the IRS tax codes or know how to execute investment options to understand "how" the Financial Pocketknife® is beneficial and the value of it.

Instead of learning boring technical jargon, surveys show that people typically just want simplicity.

When it comes to buying life insurance, 83% of consumers state that "easy to understand" is very or extremely important. (LIMRA 2016)

Due to the desire of simplicity, the primary goal of this book is to make the "complex" simple!
While some features of "The Financial Pocketknife" can be very complex, which I do cover in detail, I am more focused on the "conceptual" understanding of the strategy. I have also included several metaphors, used simple wording to describe

16

features and segmented technical information to better align with different learning styles.

🂠 Nerd Alert!

To address different learning preferences, I have posted "Nerd Alerts" throughout the book. For those of you who like to know the technical details of a subject, you will see boxed sections with additional information on the topic being discussed. For those of you who are more high-level minded, you can skip these sections at your pleasure (although I recommend everyone know the details). And for those of you wondering: No, the icon is not a caricature of me, although I proudly consider myself part nerd.

In today's "information society", we are overwhelmed by all the information from banks, insurance companies, news channels, books, publications, friends, family, accountants, attorneys and advisors. And, funny enough, they all have different theories with little consensus on the best practice for any given topic. Most of us are too busy raising families, going to school, building a career or just living life, to sift through all this information – much less monitor all of our financial interests.

Because of today's time demands, the style of this book was designed to be narrow in focus, maximize delivery of information and minimize your time investment. Some chapters may be small because I don't want to add fluff for the sake of filling space. I don't like reading books like that, and I am guessing you don't either. Just like any journey, you must begin by taking the first step, so let's get started!

Chapter 1

The Goal – Life, Not Numbers

All our dreams can come true, if we have the courage to pursue them.

Walt Disney

We all have dreams! Some of us may have given up on our dreams, but we all have them and they are all individually unique. Some may dream of becoming the President of the United States or traveling in space while others may have more humble dreams of owning a home, starting a business or traveling to Rome.

Dreams are uniquely human and provide the power to overcome seemingly insurmountable obstacles. Dreams motivate us to go beyond what we thought we were capable of. They allow us to build magnificent structures, travel through space, overcome oppression, find new worlds, discover medical breakthroughs, invent new technologies, create impactful art and raise our families. They supply us with courage we didn't know we had and give us a reason to be persistent even when it feels like the world is crumbling down around us. Without dreams and hope, our lives are empty.

As children, we all had grandiose dreams. There were no restrictions. We had dreams of being a famous rock singer, movie star, professional athlete, a prominent doctor, president or astronaut. Nobody, not a single person, says as a 10-year-old kid that they want to grow up working a 9-to-5 job, live paycheck to paycheck, retire at 65, play bingo and die in their sleep by themselves!

But then something happens. As we grow up, we are attacked by Dream Killers, and slowly we lose our hope. We lose our ability to dream and we settle for a life of survival. Before we know it, we are working a 9-to-5 job and living paycheck to paycheck. Our biggest dreams morph into winning the lottery or hoping that one day we won't have to work our 9-to-5 job and be able to retire.

I recently sought advice from a pastor friend of mine who helps families deal with all kinds of tragedies and hardships. I asked him what to say to comfort people in times of need. He told me that there are never perfect words to express but the one constant is that people are looking for "hope." They want to know that regardless of the circumstances, there is hope that things will somehow be okay. That the dreams they have can still be true. That the life they envisioned is still possible.

While the content of this book is focused on financial topics, the purpose of the book is not about numbers or financial strategies. Rather, it is about the fulfillment of dreams. It is popular in the financial industry to calculate a magical number that people need to retire or achieve a goal. And once you achieve your number, you are presumably set. While I agree calculations are important, I think focusing on numbers makes us miss the bigger picture of life and its purpose. It's an absolute fact of life that dreams and personal finance are dependent on one another, but I know a lot of wealthy people who are very unhappy and not fulfilled.

The objective shouldn't be achieving a number, the objective should be how to live a fulfilled life and achieve our dreams. When you think in terms of dreams rather than numbers, you internalize your mission and seek it with greater purpose. This is an important concept to understand as we progress through the following chapters as you will notice many of the points are not financial but rather thoughts to help you beat the Dream Killers and enhance your chances of achieving your dreams.

By the way, the "magical number" from a financial planning perspective is only part of a strong plan. It does not consider many of the risks we will be discussing, and therefore, is limited in practice. Also, when you focus on your dreams rather than the numbers, you find that the numbers needed to fulfill those dreams become bigger as your vision expands. Bigger numbers are not a bad thing, just an indication of bigger dreams!

While the variables in achieving your dreams are great and there is not a magic wand to make them happen or any way to guarantee them, I can emphatically, without doubt, guarantee you two things about successfully achieving your dreams.

First, dreams do not come without a cost! No significant dream has been achieved without blood, sweat, tears, sacrifice, time or financial commitment. The older I get and the more wisdom I obtain, the more I realize that hard work is generally the number one ingredient to success. There is a saying that "Hard work beats talent when talent doesn't work hard." I agree! You must understand, embrace and plan on this truth.

The second guarantee is that no one else is going to be responsible for you achieving your dreams. YOU, and YOU ALONE are responsible for YOUR dreams. This doesn't mean that others aren't going to help. In fact, most big dreams require the help of others. What it does mean is that you are not going to wake up one morning and look out the window to see the skies have parted and all your dreams have landed in a pile of gold at the end of a rainbow.

You have to make things happen. You have to have the discipline to plan and sacrifice. You have to keep going when things get tough and pivot when needed. You have to resist the negativity of others. You have to fight the Dream Killers! BUT ... YOU get the satisfaction and sense of accomplishment when you overcome all the obstacles to achieve YOUR dreams!

Dream Planning

It may seem simple enough, but the first step in achieving your dreams is to define them. We all have dreams that we think about throughout the day, but very few of us take the time to actually sit down and formally develop a plan. In fact, studies suggest that most people spend more time planning their vacation than planning their dreams. Think about that! Aren't your life and dreams as important as figuring out which hotel you are going to stay in? It has also been proven that you are more likely to achieve your dreams when you write them down and review them on a regular basis. After all, how can you ever reach your goals if you haven't defined your goals? As an analogy, how could you get in your car and drive to your destination if you don't know where your destination is?

The 6 Fs

There are many thoughts on dream planning, but I subscribe to the "6 Fs" method. The 6 Fs represent:

- Faith
- Family
- Friends
- Finance
- Fitness
- Fun

While there have been variations on these elements, I borrowed the foundation of this thought process from my good friend Dave Zillig, who incorporates these Fs in his *Equilibrium* program. The fundamental thought of this program is that one must be balanced in these areas to have a fulfilling life. And, when you focus too much on one area, it is often at the expense of the others – which, in turn, takes you out of "equilibrium" and leads to detrimental results.

I added a sixth F to the Equilibrium program with "Fun" and incorporated a cost and time component. The "Fun" component does not imply that you don't have fun with the other components, but rather that there are dreams you have in life that are simply for the experience itself. For example, you may want to jump out of an airplane or visit Australia.

I urge you to go through the exercise of planning your dreams and believe you will find it very impactful. Refer to the Appendix for a template of the Dream Planner or download a free copy on our website at www.thefinancialpocketknife.com. Keep in mind, you want to be as specific as possible. Define your dreams in such a way that they are quantifiable and have timelines and costs. We will talk about this more in Chapter 12, *Putting It All Together*.

Chapter 2

Defining the Enemy, the Dream Killers

Know your enemy and know yourself, and you can fight a hundred battles without disaster.

Sun Tzu

If our goal is to win the battle of financial independence and achieve our dreams, we need to know who our enemies are. In a broad sense, I refer to our opponents as Dream Killers! After all, the occurrence of these life challenges dramatically affects our ability to fulfill our individual dreams.

In some cases, these elements are financial, but not always. In fact, my experience has been that non-financial issues (e.g., procrastination) are the biggest reason why people fail to accomplish their goals.

For simplicity, I have developed the ***Dream Killer Risk Quadrant™*** *(DKRQ)*. The DKRQ is a visual reference tool designed to easily identify and categorize Dream Killers and demonstrate how effective the Financial Pocketknife® is at combatting each risk.

Dream Killers can be categorized into four quadrants:

- Physical
- Financial
- Environmental
- Personal

While not comprehensive of all life risks, the DKRQs cover many significant risks that inhibit individuals and families from achieving their life goals.

Although outside the scope of this book, it is imperative that individuals also understand and manage general health and property risks (e.g., via health insurance, property and casualty, etc.).

While many of the Dream Killer terms are self-evident, it is important that we define each term individually to ensure consistency, identify the scope of the threat and fully understand the positive impact of the Financial Pocketknife®.

Physical Risks represent risks to one's physical body which either inhibit one's ability to produce income and/or create substantial expenses that diminish monetary assets.

Financial Risks are those risks at the "micro" (individual) level that directly relate to one's monetary assets.

Environmental Risks refer to "macro" level events in which one has little to no ability to control.

Finally, Personal Risks are those risks that are not directly related to financial issues at all, but rather personal attitudes and behaviors which create financial (or other life) challenges.

While you may already understand the definition of many of the risks in the DKRQ, let's take a quick minute to review:

Quadrant I – Physical Risks

Death

As obvious as the definition of death is, many people (especially young and healthy) don't realize the incredible financial impact it has on one's family. Today, the average North American traditional funeral costs between $7,000 and $10,000. (Parting.com). Not only does a family have to bear the costs of burial, but they also forgo ALL future earnings the decedent would have made if alive. While the loss of income can equal hundreds of thousands of dollars, those who have witnessed the devastation that families suffer when a breadwinner dies understand that it is something that no one should ever have to go through. Literally, it can cause unbearable distress for a family that can have a rippling effect for generations.

Critical Illness

A 25-year-old male non-smoker has a 24% chance of having a critical illness (cancer, heart attack or stroke) prior to turning age 65. The same-aged male who smokes has a 49% chance, according to a National Critical Illness Risk Assessment Study published by the American Association for Critical Illness Insurance.

"Cancer, heart attacks and strokes happen at all ages and most people are not prepared for either the emotional or financial cost," explains Jesse Slome, executive director of the industry trade organization. "Nearly two-thirds of U.S. bankruptcies are the result of medical expenses and 78% of those filing for bankruptcy had health insurance when they were first diagnosed."

It is very important that you review the coverage listed by the company offering the coverage, but depending on the company, critical illness generally includes major heart attack, coronary artery bypass, stroke, invasive cancer, blood cancers (leukemia, lymphoma, multiple myeloma), major organ transplant, end stage renal failure, paralysis, coma and severe burn.

Chronic Illness

- As of 2012, about half of all adults – 117 million people – had one or more chronic health conditions. One in four adults had two or more chronic health conditions.
- Seven of the top 10 causes of death in 2014 were chronic diseases. Two of these chronic diseases – heart disease and cancer – together accounted for nearly 46% of all deaths. (Centers for Disease Control and Prevention)

Although companies may differ with their definition and coverage, typically a chronic illness is an illness or physical condition which permanently affects an individual so that he or she:

Is unable to perform at least two of the six Activities of Daily Living (bathing, dressing, toileting, transferring, continence and eating) without substantial assistance; or

Requires substantial supervision by another person to protect an individual from threats to health and safety due to severe cognitive impairment – and for which the individual is under a plan of care prescribed by a licensed health care practitioner.

And, the cost can be staggering! The average cost today for a private room is about $97,400 per year and the average stay in a skilled nursing facility is about 2.5 years. If you do the math, this means a person entering a nursing home today could expect to pay over $243,000 for the full term of his or her care. With inflation (another Dream Killer), a 2.5-year stay may cost almost $400,000 ten years from now (assuming 5% increase in cost per year, higher than the traditional rate of inflation).

Just think, you've carefully planned, saved, and sacrificed for your family and dreams only to find you lose it all to the expenses of Chronic Illness.

Disability

Disability is defined as a physical or mental impairment that substantially limits one or more major life activities. A disability may inhibit an individual from being able to work for a period of time, sometimes permanently. Moreover, one has a much greater chance of becoming disabled in his or her lifetime than dying prematurely. Yet, disability insurance is rarely a point of focus for most people. To make it worse, disability can be a double whammy as expenses can go way up while income can be erased.

- Just over 1 in 4 of today's 20-year-olds will become disabled before they retire.
- Over 37 million Americans are classified as disabled – about 12% of the total population. More than 50% of those disabled Americans are in their working years, from 18-64.
- 8.8 million disabled wage earners, over 5% of U.S. workers, were receiving Social Security Disability (SSDI) benefits at the end of 2012.
- In December of 2012, there were over 2.5 million disabled workers in their 20s, 30s and 40s receiving SSDI benefits. (Council for Disability Awareness)

Live Too Long

Living too long is a recent phenomenon which Americans now have to take into great consideration when preparing their financial plan. It's hard to imagine that in 1900, life expectancy was only 47.3 years, and in the 1930s (Social Security was founded in 1935) it was 58 for men and 62 for women. Today, with a life expectancy of approximately 78, one may live 13-20 years **after** the traditional retirement age of 65.

Odds are almost one in three that a 65-year-old man will live to age 90 and about one in eight that he'll live until age 95 – 11 years beyond his life expectancy. A 65-year-old woman has 42% odds of living to age 90, and 21% odds (more than one in five) of living to age 95 – nine years beyond her life expectancy. (American Academy of Actuaries)

As a result, there is great risk that one may outlive his or her assets. To add insult to injury, it's very unlikely that one will have the ability to work at full capacity to earn additional income at an older age.

Quadrant II – Financial Risks

Inflation

Inflation is the rate at which the general level of prices for goods and services is rising, and subsequently, purchasing power is falling. Central banks attempt to stop severe inflation, along with severe deflation, in an attempt to keep the excessive growth of prices to a minimum. (Investopedia)

Have you ever heard your parents or grandparents complain about how much something costs? Normally, it goes something like "Back in the day, gas only cost 25 cents a gallon" or "I used to buy a Coke for a dime." This can be very annoying until you realize one day that the old geezer complaining is you. Were things really that cheap? That depends on how you define cheap. If you define it by the amount of money it took to buy an item, you may consider it cheap, but it doesn't really matter what the price of something is, rather it matters what the price is relative to your income.

You see, the old geezer complaining about the price of a Coke often fails to give you the other side of the equation, which was his salary. If the geezer made $6,186 in 1970, then spending 10 cents on a soft drink was equivalent to spending $1.50 today.

Market Risk

Market risk is the possibility for an investor to experience losses due to factors that affect the overall performance of the financial markets. Market risk, also called "systematic risk," cannot be eliminated through diversification, though it can be hedged against. (Investopedia)

Many of us who had stock market investments during the past 20 years are very familiar with market risk as great wealth was erased in a relatively short period of time.

The dot-com bubble of 2000 caused the market to decline 49.1% in 30 months, while the burst of the housing bubble in 2007 caused the market to free fall 56.4% in 17 months. For those of us young enough, it took years for our accounts to recover, but for those in or near retirement, many were ruined financially and were never able to recover.

Taxes

Taxation refers to the act of a taxing authority actually levying tax. Taxation as a term applies to all types of taxes, from income to gift to estate taxes. It is usually referred to as an act; any revenue collected is usually called "taxes."

As we will learn, taxes can significantly affect our quality of life. Many people are shocked to find out that Tax Freedom Day, the first day Americans are collectively able to work for themselves instead of working to pay taxes, is in late April (31% of the nation's income in 2015 per the Tax Foundation). However, you WILL NOT BELIEVE the highest income tax rates in U.S. history, which we will cover later. You may want to write down your guess on the side of the page and see how close you are, but don't ruin it now by peeking.

Liquidity

Liquidity is the risk stemming from the lack of marketability of an investment that cannot be bought or sold quickly enough to prevent or minimize a loss.

Typically, one does not think about liquidity being a challenge, but it can be a huge problem. When the mortgage crisis occurred in the 2000s, liquidity became highlighted as people had hundreds of thousands (even millions) of dollars held in real estate that was illiquid. Many of us recall having houses we could not sell and banks that would not make home equity loans. If we were able to sell, it was for a big loss.

Debt

Debt is an epidemic in America! The average consumer has 13 credit obligations, and the average household credit card debt is $8,377. As we will discuss, not all debt is bad, but bad debt is really bad. It traps people into a life of surviving instead of thriving while credit card companies push credit cards on us like a street thug pushes narcotics.

When you get in debt you become a slave.

Andrew Jackson

Despite this epidemic, I'm not one who believes in being totally debt free. I maintain that there is good debt and bad debt. This may be controversial and against prevalent preaching from the radio gurus I know, but I will explain in detail why debt can be good and how "The Financial Pocketknife®" can help with this issue in the chapters to come.

For now, we just need to know that bad debt kills dreams!

Cash Flow

Cash Flow is generally used as a management tool for businesses. For our purposes, however, we are referring to personal cash flow which includes:

- Salaries, pension distributions, interest from savings accounts, dividends from investments, capital gains from the sale of financial securities such as stocks and bonds, social security payments and alimony

Cash inflow can also include money received from the sale of assets like houses or cars. Essentially, your cash inflow consists of anything that brings in money.

Cash Flow has elements of other risks including Debt and Liquidity but is distinct because it focuses on income and expenses. Typically, this Dream Killer occurs due to overspending and/or excessive debt but can also be due to under-employment.

Quadrant III – Environmental Risks

Some things are just out of our control.

Environmental Risk refers to those risks in our external environment which we are triggered by people and/or events other than yourself. While outside our span of control, these events can have a devastating impact.

Life Emergency

There aren't many guarantees in life but you can take it to the bank that if you live long enough, you will have a Life Emergency that you did not expect and at a time that you can't control.

In our definition of Life Emergency, I am referring to non-catastrophic events which occur on a fairly regular basis which may cost $1,000 to $5,000 depending on your income level and circumstance. Perhaps you lose a tooth and need a bone graph not covered by insurance that costs in excess of $6,000 (yes, that is a personal example). Maybe your business has to close down for a week due to a hurricane threat, (yes, another personal example) or your car blows its engine (I will let you guess on that one!). These events can create unforeseen hardships that provide major setbacks for your financial goals.

According to a 2017 GOBankingRates survey, more than half of Americans (57%) have less than $1,000 in their savings accounts.

Legal Issues

Think that you are immune from a Legal Issue? Think again. With more than 16,000,000 civil law suits filed each year in state courts alone and the highest lawyer population in the world, you are a target. Whether you win the lawsuit or not, the expenses alone can be catastrophic. Just review these stats by Statistic Brain:

Civil Lawsuit Statistics	Data
Annual cost to the US economy for civil lawsuits	$239,000,000,000
Estimated annual cost to each U.S. citizen for civil lawsuits	$812
% of people who believe advertising by personal-injury lawyers encourages people to sue, even if they have not been injured	79%
Average compensation payout for injury lawsuits	$60,000
% of punitive damages suits won by plaintiff	6%
Average awarded in a punitive damage lawsuit	$50,000

Poor Economy

A recession – defined by the National Bureau of Economic Research (NBER) Business Cycle Dating Committee, the group entrusted to call the start and end dates of a recession – is "a significant decline in economic activity spread across the economy, lasting more than a few months." (Investopedia)

If you have lived through a recession as a working adult, you understand how difficult times can be. If you have not lived through a recession, you will. Layoffs happen as companies downsize; poor economy can lead to chaos. But you don't have to get laid off to be affected by a poor economy. You may lose income through lost bonuses or revenue if you are a business owner. You may lose value in your home or not be able to sell a house. You may lose rental income as tenants lose their jobs. Or, you may lose market value in your retirement investments.

While the term recession comes to mind when we think about a poor economy, there are also issues that can cause challenges in a strong economy. Inflation can run rampant and borrowing rates can soar among other challenges.

Recession is when your neighbor loses his job.

Depression is when you lose yours.

Ronald Reagan

Job Loss

Although job loss can often be attributed to a poor economy, it can include many other scenarios as well. Your job could be outsourced, your company may relocate, the functions you perform could be automated, or you just may have a new boss who wants to shake things up and bring his own team.

Along with the death of a loved one and divorce, social scientists rank job loss as a top factor of stress and depression. Considering the alarming statistics we have shared regarding U.S. savings habits, the job loss of a primary breadwinner can have a rippling and exponential effect. You may lose your house, workplace benefits and even your marriage as we will see in the Divorce risk.

Quadrant IV – Personal Risks

Lack of Knowledge

Not understanding financial issues and not knowing what you don't know can have horrific effects on your family dreams and goals. I constantly see people who have made costly financial mistakes that could have easily been avoided with a little education.

Perhaps they take out a loan with bad terms, fail to insure themselves for a catastrophic event, invest their money into an overly risky investment or needlessly spend money on a service they didn't need.

Regardless of the situation, there is an expense for having Lack of Knowledge when it comes to personal finance, and many times it can cripple your dreams as a result.

Divorce

Depending on how it is measured, between 35% and 50% of marriages end in divorce. According to Forbes, the average cost of divorce is between $15,000 and $30,000. It can truly be a Dream Killer in many significant ways.

Almost half of American families experience poverty following a divorce, and 75% of all women who apply for welfare benefits do so because of a disrupted marriage or a disrupted relationship in which they live with a male outside of marriage. (Marripedia)

While Divorce may not be a topic one would normally see in a book based on financial issues, it should be. Not only does it wreck people emotionally, but it can have a devastating financial impact.

Fear

Think about a time in your life where you avoided doing something you wanted to do because of fear. Notice that I didn't ask you "if" you had this experience but assumed that you did. The reason is that we, as humans, all have had this experience, and most of us regret it at some point in the future. The truth is that other than Death, Fear is the biggest Dream Killer for most of us. We are not born to live in fear but rather are conditioned to be fearful. Ironically, fear is a function of information, or lack thereof, and typically an overreaction to an assumed danger. One thing is for sure: to achieve our dreams, we will have to battle this Dream Killer.

Procrastination

In my professional experience, Procrastination (lack of discipline) may be the single largest inhibitor to one's financial success. I have often met with people who continually "put things off for another day" and before they know it, they have missed 30 years of savings, passed away without life insurance, did not fund their child's college tuition, or even begin an emergency fund. Unfortunately, they call me when it is too late. While I certainly assist them however I can, I can't bring a dead person back to life, replace 30 years of savings, or snap my fingers and make tuition appear. I'm a financial advisor, not a magician.

I would include a lack of attentiveness in the category of Procrastination. Sometimes, one will take action and implement a strategy but will not be attentive to the details of the strategy or monitor it afterward for challenges. This lack of attentiveness can cause much pain.

Note: Health Issues and Real Property Loss

As stated in the Preface, I fully recognize that health issues can be a significant challenge as can property loss (e.g., car totaled from accident or a house fire). These risks are not included in the DKRQ for a couple of reasons. First and foremost, P&C (property and casualty) and health insurance are mandated coverages in most circumstances by law and lenders, so the risk diminishes. Secondly, elements of both are covered in other identified risks such as Critical and Chronic Illness.

Now that we know our enemies and their significant power to kill our dreams, as the great Chinese war leader Sun Tsu advised, it is time to go fight for our dreams. And, to be clear, it is a fight! And if we want to win our fight, we better have some powerful weapons and know how to use them!

Chapter 3
Wax On, Wax Off

First learn stand, then learn fly. Nature rule, Daniel-san, not mine.
Mr. Miyagi

In "The Karate Kid" (the original good one, not the remake), the karate sensei, Mr. Miyagi, instructs his student, Daniel, to wash his cars and then put wax on them. He tells him to spread the wax on in a circular motion with his right hand and then rub the wax off in a circular motion with his left hand. Then he repeats his little mantra, "Wax on, wax off."

Most of us know the rest of the story. Daniel gets very frustrated with waxing cars and has a temper tantrum with Mr. Miyagi complaining that he is supposed to be learning karate, not waxing cars. Ultimately, he learns that the waxing motion was used to develop muscle memory for self-defense and a drill for blocking. The bigger lesson to be learned was that you have to learn the basics before your can become a champion.

I suspect at this point in the book, you are wanting to have all the mysteries of "The Financial Pocketknife®" revealed, but hang in there with me. We need to review a few financial concepts to get the most benefit from the chapters to come. Even if you are a financial professional or consider yourself a more advanced consumer, take the time to review this chapter.

FUN-damentals

I am a huge fan of baseball and have coached teams from the T-Ball level through high school. One of my favorite things to watch is the Little League World Series. I love watching kids who play for the love of the game compete to be the most successful in the world. While I always root for the U.S.A., I love watching the

Japanese teams. From 2000-2015, they have won six World Championships and have been runner-up four times.

What is really interesting when you watch the Japanese kids is that they are typically the smallest athletes in the tournament. No 6-foot, 200-pound, 12-year-olds throwing 70+ miles per hour. Instead, you will see these little 5-foot, 60-pound kids dominating the tournament. While they are certainly talented, they are not as big and strong as their competition. They aren't as fast or athletic. However, they just win all the time. How do they pull this off? On paper, they should have no chance.

The key to Team Japan's success is the mastering of fundamentals. They understand how to play the game and how to execute the basics needed to win. Specifically, they focus their training on throwing with the correct form, batting with the proper stance, catching with the right technique, and most importantly, what to do with the ball in every situation. They very rarely make a mistake and as a result, execute their game plan flawlessly. Because of this mastery of fundamentals, they are very successful and have a lot of FUN. As the saying goes, "there is no Fun without the Fundamentals."

Like baseball (and most life endeavors), financial success comes from understanding and successfully executing the fundamentals. To truly appreciate the benefits and value of "The Financial Pocketknife," you must first understand a few fundamentals of personal financial planning.

While there are over 13,000 terms in Investopedia's financial dictionary, which is obviously overwhelming to most everyone, we really just need to remember a very simple premise for financial success:

You need to make as much money as you can AND avoid losses as much as possible.

I realize this is not an Einsteinian revelation, but again the fundamental purpose of this book is to make the complex simple. The trick of course is to understand "the how." How do we make as much as we can, and how do we avoid losing the money we accumulate?

The answer of "how" is complicated, of course. There are literally thousands of books in the world professing how, encompassing many areas of study, many theories and many practices.

Despite the myriad of information and opinions, there is no one perfect answer or practice for everyone. There is no magic formula for guaranteed success and even the most successful people will often admit that their success was based on many different factors, including a little luck.

There are, however, some undeniable mathematic truths to make money and build wealth. The amount of wealth one will ultimately accumulate is based on:

1) Savings Amount
2) Investment Returns
3) Time Period

Savings

"Savings" is the amount of money you put aside on a regular basis for future use. It is the amount of money you have left after paying for all of your expenses. The challenge is that most Americans don't do a very good job of saving.

Whether you like it or not, you are one or the other! You are either a saver or a borrower. A very successful business man I worked for as a college student had a great axiom on creating a successful business, which also applies to the practice of saving:

Rule # 1 - Make more money than you spend.

Rule # 2 - Spend less money than you make.

This seems simple enough doesn't it? But why don't the majority of Americans follow this rule? The answer really has nothing to do with technical financial reasons, it has more to do with culture and behavior. We live in the wealthiest country in the history of the world where the average person today has a greater standard of living than kings and queens 200 years ago. And while the income gap in the U.S. continues to grow, the typical person in the bottom 5% of the American income distribution is still richer than 68% of the world's inhabitants. (Forbes)

Yet, the U.S. savings rate of 2.4% is among the lowest in the world. For comparison, here's how our savings rate compares to much of the developed world:

- o U.S. Savings Rate = 2.4% in 2016 vs 11.1% in 1985 (Fed)
- o Europe = 20%
- o Japan = 25%
- o China = 50%

These numbers are shocking! The lack of personal savings by Americans may be our largest national problem and certainly the least talked about. What happens when the "generation of spending and debt" tries to retire? (Note, I stated "tries", not "wants.") What if Social Security is unstable as math would suggest? What do you think the government will do with tax rates when we have a large part of the country's voting block struggling with retirement?

I will let you dwell on those questions as the answers could be the subject of a book by itself, but suffice it to say that it won't be pretty (and taxes are unlikely to go down). I vehemently believe it is wise to have a savings plan of your own and embrace the need to save with a great sense of urgency. The simple fact of the matter is that if you don't save, you are sentencing yourself and your family to a life of struggle and killing your dreams!

When most people talk about how to increase savings, they typically focus on developing a budget and finding ways to minimize expenses. This practice is an absolute must, but not within the scope of this book. There are many ways to reduce expenses and abundant educational material readily available on this topic. I will say, however, that technology is your friend. In today's advanced world, creating and monitoring a budget does not have to be difficult. There are several low-cost, user-friendly and secure web applications that allow you to create a budget, pay your bills and monitor expenses. There is zero excuse not to have a budget tool these days.

While expenses are important, a great mentor of mine used to share that revenue (income) can always solve a bad budget and hide expense problems. My challenge to you is to make sure that you don't assume your income is fixed, but rather consider ways to increase your income. Perhaps you invest in additional education for yourself, take on a second job or start a side business. The main point is that you need to focus on both sides of the equation (income and expenses), rather than just one (expenses).

Again, you must understand first and foremost, above all, without a doubt, the single most important element of saving successfully is personal income. Unless you are already independently wealthy or have a lifetime income stream from a family trust, your earned income ultimately is going to dictate your ability to save and quality of life.

Bottom line: you must earn money AND save it!

Investment Returns

If you have ever worked in a corporate environment, you are probably familiar with the annual review and raise process. Most employees are typically disappointed when they dedicate their time and talent to a company, get a strong review and then get the "good" news that they will receive a 2-3% raise for the following year. This 2% isn't very motivating and gets even worse when you get your next paycheck and see that you also had to pay taxes on the 2%. And when we consider inflation, there is a good chance that you didn't actually receive any real benefit. Instead, you simply didn't lose money for doing a great job.

We will discuss the importance of inflation a little later in the book, but for now I want to share how important a seemingly small difference in return can be extremely valuable and why you should be excited about how powerful a simple 2% increase in return can actually be, especially in relation to investing.

Take a look at our illustration below comparing Sister A to Sister B. In this example, we compare the returns of two sisters investing $2,400 per year into an account over a 30-year period. Sister A earns an 8% return while Sister B receives a 6% return, or 2% less. In the left- hand column of each example, the annual contribution of $2,400 is reflected while the right- hand column displays the accumulation of all contributions plus returns.

Only a 2 % Difference?
Rate of Return Matters: 8% vs. 6%

	Sister A @ 8%		Sister B @ 6%	
1	2,400	2,592	2,400	2,544
2	2,400	5,391	2,400	5,241
3	2,400	8,415	2,400	8,099
4	2,400	11,680	2,400	11,129
5	2,400	15,206	2,400	14,341
6	2,400	19,015	2,400	17,745
7	2,400	23,128	2,400	21,354
8	2,400	27,570	2,400	25,179
9	2,400	32,368	2,400	29,234
10	2,400	37,549	2,400	33,532
11	2,400	43,145	2,400	38,088
12	2,400	49,189	2,400	42,917
13	2,400	55,716	2,400	48,036
14	2,400	62,765	2,400	53,462
15	2,400	70,378	2,400	59,214
16	2,400	78,601	2,400	65,311
17	2,400	87,481	2,400	71,774
18	2,400	97,071	2,400	78,624
19	2,400	107,429	2,400	85,885
20	2,400	118,615	2,400	93,583
21	2,400	130,696	2,400	101,741
22	2,400	143,744	2,400	110,390
23	2,400	157,835	2,400	119,557
24	2,400	173,054	2,400	129,275
25	2,400	189,491	2,400	139,575
26	2,400	207,242	2,400	150,494
27	2,400	226,413	2,400	162,067
28	2,400	247,118	2,400	174,336
29	2,400	269,480	2,400	187,340
30	2,400	**293,630**	2,400	**201,124**
	72,000		72,000	
2% Difference in Dollars			92,506	
2% Difference as a % of Total			46%	

Most people are amazed at how a seemingly small difference in interest rate can make such a huge difference in total returns over time. Because Sister A receives 2% more annually than Sister B over a 30-year period, she ends up with $92,506 more. That's 46% more than Sister B.

The lesson here is that small increments can make a huge difference. But as an extension of this lesson, we should understand two more facts. First, when analyzing returns, it is important to understand a nominal return versus a real return. A nominal return is the amount earned before any direct or implicit costs while the real return is the amount that you "really" receive. For example, in our previous scenario of a 2% raise, I mentioned that after inflation, you might just break even. Think about it: if you get a 2% raise but inflation (the cost of goods and services) goes up 2%, you really didn't gain anything. Your nominal return was 2% but your real return was 0%.

The second fact is that because small percentages can add up, you need to be sensitive to investment expenses because they can become significant over time. And while investment charges and sales fees are often cited, taxes and opportunity cost can be much more expensive as we will see.

It is important to understand that investment returns can refer to several things, including interest, capital appreciation and dividends. Investment returns can be difficult to measure because they are reported in different ways. Some reporting may include or exclude taxes. Some may or may not include expenses. In keeping with our theme of simplicity, I won't cover all these technicalities but want you to always have this idea in the back of your mind so you can compare apples to apples. Normally, any illustrations showing returns will state what is included in the fine print.

Time

Obviously, the greater return one gets on his investment, the greater his money grows. But what people often don't realize is the amount of time your investment has to grow can be significantly more important that your actual rate of return. This is due to compound interest. Albert Einstein stated that the most powerful force in the universe is compound interest, as we can see in our previous chart (Sister A vs. Sister B).

Notice that in our 8% scenario, while Sister A invested $72,000, she earned $221,630 in total returns. And in the last year, while she only contributed $2,400, she earned an additional $21,750 in compounded interest. I have saved a detailed illustration of compound interest for an impactful segment at the end of the book, but I think you get the point in this example, that Time is incredibly important. Because of this, starting a savings plan as soon as possible may be the greatest thing you can do long term to accumulate wealth.

Rule of 72, a Cool Trick

The "Rule of 72" is a simplified way to determine how long an investment will take to double in value, given a fixed annual rate of interest. By dividing 72 by the annual rate of return, investors can get a rough estimate of how many years it will take for the initial investment to duplicate itself. For example, if you invested $100 at 8% annually, it would take you approximately nine years for your investment to grow to $200. (72 ÷ 8 = 9)

Once It Is Made, Don't Lose It

In all my years of studying highly technical financial concepts, the most important lesson I have ever learned is to avoid losing money. In fact, Warren Buffet, recognized as one of the best investors of all time (the Michael Jordon of investing), is credited with this axiom:

RULE # 1 - DON'T LOSE MONEY

RULE # 2 - NEVER FORGET RULE # 1

Warren Buffett

The postulate of "Not Losing Money" is such an important concept because, mathematically, it is more important NOT TO have a negative return than it is to have a positive return. For example, if you were to lose 50% on an investment, most people don't understand that they would have to receive a 100% return (not a 50%) return just to get back to your original balance.

🤓 **Nerd Alert!**
Doing the Math
1. Original Account Value = $100
2. Account loses 50%, Value of Account is now $50
3. Scenario 1: Market returns 50%. New Account Value is $75.
4. Scenario 2: Market returns 100%. New Account Value is $100.

	Original	Scenario 1	Scenario 2
Value of Account	$100	$50	$50
Market Gain/Loss	- 50%	50%	100%
New Value	$50	$75	$100

This example is for conceptual purposes only and is not intended to show actual/potential market returns.

While we generally associate losing money with "market risk," the reality is that investment loss is only one way to lose money. In fact, if we look at our *Dream Killer Risk Quadrant,* most of the killers represent ways of losing money. For example, Taxes, Inflation, loss of income due to Critical Illness, and Legal Issues are just a few that can lead to substantial losses. Many times, these losses can be even greater than any market loss.

The practice of minimizing or eliminating risk is referred to as Risk Management. And while there are many methods used in the practice of risk management, insurance is by far the most used tool. As we will see, insurance can be used in many creative ways, including market risk, taxes and critical illness just to name a few.

Insurance Evolution

You may have a few yawns as we address this section, but to maximize your understanding of the concepts in this book, it is important that you know the basics of life insurance. The origin of life insurance, as we know it, can be traced to ancient Rome. Caius Marius, a Roman military leader, created a burial club among his troops, so in the event of the unexpected death of a club member, other members would pay for the funeral expenses (Thinkadvisor).

Over time, the concept of a saving component was added to life insurance with the idea that life insurance would help build wealth and create retirement income for families. For years, life insurance was the primary vehicle used for accumulating wealth, and as I mentioned in the Pregame, it was used by Walt Disney to help fund his empire and by other iconic business titans for capital.

Life insurance has evolved over the years to include all kinds of benefits that the Romans could have never of dreamed. As a result, life insurance companies offer products in many different forms with many different benefits. Because of the numerous life insurance products offered, consumers can easily get overwhelmed by all the different types. However, these products can be simplified by making a distinction between Term and Cash Value insurance.

"Term" insurance is by far the simplest form of life insurance. As its name suggests, term insurance remains active for a specified time period, or term. For example, you might purchase a 30-year term policy for the purpose of protecting a breadwinner for a 30-year mortgage. At the end of the term, the contract is completed, and coverage ceases.

"Cash Value" life insurance has a savings component (cash) in addition to the insurance component. Significantly, it typically does not have a set term but rather is "permanent" insurance. In other words, it does not expire after a specific term but is designed to last for the entire life of the insured (calculated as high as 121 years old). Most of the various life insurance product types fall under the cash value insurance category.

Although the terms are often used interchangeably, permanent life insurance, cash value life insurance and whole life insurance can represent many different types of policies. For purposes of the book, the terms "permanent" and "cash value" may be used interchangeably. The term "Whole Life," however, should not be used interchangeably because it is a type of cash value policy based on a fixed investment option, not a category by itself.

Financial Advisor vs. Agent

Financial professionals are always coming up with new titles to call themselves. While the term "Agent" is usually designated for one who solicits insurance and "Financial Advisor" typically connotes a greater emphasis on investments (and additional licensing), we will use the terms interchangeably as both typically promote life insurance in planning.

Financial Foundation

As we close our chapter on fundamentals, I want to stress the need to create a financial foundation. Just as the Japanese little league pitchers must master throwing fastballs for strikes before they are taught curve balls and sliders, we need to first develop a strong financial foundation before we focus on other tools. Remember, The Financial Pocketknife is a tool to create a financial foundation.

Foundation: the basis or groundwork of anything

Chapter 4
The Financial Pocketknife®

If you can't explain it simply, then you don't understand it well enough.
Albert Einstein

Conceptual before Technical

As a college professor, I've learned that people learn in different ways. Some may be visual learners, some may be hands-on, and some are readers. One common denominator among any method, however, is that adults typically learn technical material easier once they have a conceptual understanding of the subject before drilling down into the technical details. The conceptual teaching explains the "Why" (why we do something) question before the "How" (how we do it).

A great example of this idea was when McDonald's introduced the very first drive-through in China. As much as this concept is second nature to Americans, the idea of driving up to a restaurant's window and getting food was a shock to the Chinese (just as it was to Americans in the 1950s).

The first day of implementation proved very interesting for McDonald's executives as they stood in the back of the parking lot to watch the launch of the first drive-through. They noticed something very peculiar. Customers lined up in their cars, placed their order, made their payment and received their food from the restaurant's window. But then, a twist occurred. Instead of driving back out into traffic, the customers parked their car, grabbed their bagged food and walked into the restaurant to find a seat while they ate.

You see, McDonald's failed to teach the "why" first. They taught the customers "how" to navigate the drive-through but failed to explain the concept of acquiring food in an efficient, time-saving manner for the convenience and pleasure of dining elsewhere. Without the "why," it is difficult to fully understand the value of a product or service.

In the chapters to come, we will explain the details and technical aspects of the Financial Pocketknife, but in this chapter, I want you to focus on the concept. I want you to learn "why" the tool is so powerful and its underlying value from a high-level perspective. Once you understand the concept, you will then be able to better understand the details as we drill down.

The Financial Pocketknife®

I'm not a gambler, but I am willing to bet that you own a pocketknife. This would be a pretty safe bet on my part considering that 35.6 million households own one (Doublebase Mediamark Research & Intelligence). You probably haven't, however, really thought about this incredible tool in detail.

It may sound like a Seinfeld comedy sketch to make such a big deal out of something so simple, but think about it. If you were a participant on my favorite survival show, "Naked and Afraid," all by yourself in the middle of a jungle, and could only bring one item to help you survive for 21 days, can you possibly think of another item you would want more than a pocketknife? Of course not! Because it is not just one tool that has one function, but one tool that has many functions. It's a super-tool! What other singular tool is going to help you hunt for food, defend yourself from wild animals, make shelter, start a fire, pull a splinter out of your foot, create clothing or simply eat, just to name a few functions?

Of course, the knife is the primary tool in the pocketknife, but it may also have a variety of other tools, including screw drivers, tweezers, a corkscrew, a fire starter, scissors, a fish scaler, a can opener, a fork, a magnifying glass, a bottle opener or a pick. Today, some even have computer thumb drives. Together, all these individual tools add great convenience and create a powerful comprehensive super-tool for camping, everyday life and in some cases, even survival.

In our financial life, we also have a lot of different needs and use many tools to help us survive and prosper. We strive to gather resources (assets) and protect ourselves from perils to make ourselves more comfortable so we can thrive in the jungle of everyday life. Instead of knives and fire starters, we use retirement accounts and insurance. And, instead of tweezers and scissors, we may use loans and savings accounts.

And like our wilderness scenario, the financial tools we use will have a large impact on whether we thrive, survive or tap out.

Unlike our camping scenario, however, in our financial life we typically don't have a bunch of financial tools combined into one super-tool. Instead, we have a loan for our car. We have an insurance policy for our life and property. We have a savings account for our emergency loan. We have a 401(k) plan at work for our retirement. We have a mutual fund account for our kids' college. And to top it off, we typically have all these financial tools at different places with different companies and different representatives.

Wouldn't it be great if we could replicate the functionality and value that the pocketknife provides to outdoor survival in a financial tool? What if there were a "financial pocketknife"? Wouldn't the functionality and the convenience of a financial pocketknife possess tremendous value? Especially if the financial pocketknife includes exclusive tools that cannot be replicated by any one individual tool?

Shockingly, there is such a tool! For conceptual purposes, I call it the Financial Pocketknife®, but it is based on a financial product called...

INDEXED UNIVERSAL LIFE INSURANCE, OR "IUL" FOR SHORT.

While you may be familiar with some of its predecessors (Whole Life, Variable Universal Life, etc.), IUL is relatively new to the market. It is what many consider the latest and greatest evolution of life insurance. Considering life insurance has been around since Roman times, you can imagine that a lot of continuous improvement has occurred over the years just as transportation has evolved from horseback riding to driverless cars. As we will learn, Indexed Universal Life has retained all the great features from previous evolutions of life insurance products but has introduced a new technological method of managing investment options.

Now, let's address a potential "elephant in the room." For some, when they read the word "life insurance," their minds shut down. They reactively made assumptions about life insurance. They thought to themselves that they already have coverage, don't need it or really don't want to think about it because it reminds them of their own mortality. (Quick stat: the death rate has held steady at 100% for thousands of years so we all need to think about how to deal with it for our family's sake!) For others, they may harbor negative thoughts about life insurance as they conjure up images of some obnoxious salesperson stalking them (I once had to hide behind cars in a parking lot to avoid one).

If you are one of those readers who made any of these assumptions, I challenge you to suspend them for the time being and review the information that I will share with you as if you were a scientist reviewing data. Let go of any preconceived notions that may impair your ability to review the data shared in the next chapters objectively. In the end, it may prove that your assumptions were correct (you might find me to be obnoxious, too). But hopefully, if I do my job correctly, you will find that life insurance is much more than you ever imagined. Either way, it will be worth your time to learn and evaluate its merits based on the facts.

Although life insurance has been around for literally thousands of years, today,

"Life insurance is much more than insurance for your life".

Today, life insurance can provide benefits and investment options that no other financial products can offer. And while many affluent people understand these facts, the vast majority of the general public is not exposed to these concepts.

At the end this book, I believe you will agree that learning about Indexed Universal Life insurance was worth your time, and you will have reconditioned your assumptions to think of life insurance as you would a pocketknife … a valuable tool that is multifaceted and can solve many important challenges.

What's in a Name?

One reason people get anxiety over financial issues is due to the naming of products and concepts. If I were to ask you for an acetylsalicylic acid tablet, you would probably look at me cross-eyed and maybe even scoff. But, if I were to reword my request and ask for an aspirin, you might reply, "Why didn't you just say that in the first place?"

Big, fancy words often distract people from the intention and prevent effective communication. This happens many times in the medical, legal, IT and financial fields. A new language is developed and professionals often forget how to communicate with someone not in the field. And even when a term may seemingly be simple, it can often mean something else. For example, the term "bug" in relation to information technology, doesn't mean an insect.

The term "Indexed Universal Life Insurance" is one of those terms that can be very intimidating. But if we break it down, word for word, it becomes much easier. "Indexed" simply means that the savings component of the policy is tied to a stock market index (e.g., Dow, S&P). "Universal" means that the policy is flexible in terms of how much money you put into the policy, how often you fund it and how you use some of its benefits. While the term "Life Insurance" is self-explanatory, I want you to consider another way of thinking about it.

In my view, the phrase "life insurance" doesn't accurately reflect its main benefit. Life insurance doesn't ensure that you will retain your life or die of old age. Rather, it ensures that your current and future income will be protected for the benefit of your family in the event of your death. Couldn't we reasonably refer to life insurance as "income insurance" or "asset insurance"?

Combining the translated definitions of these words together, Indexed Universal Life insurance (IUL) can be thought of as:

A flexible financial product that provides a return on your savings based on a market index and protects your future income earnings when you die.

Notice our translation states "when" you die not "if" you die. The reason for this is due to IUL being a permanent policy. By permanent, I mean that the policy lasts for the entirety of your life, regardless of your age. Yes, that means if you die at 100, the insurance company will pay the death benefit to your beneficiary.

A more detailed description of Indexed Universal Life Insurance (IUL)

1. A form of permanent life insurance policy that is designed to last your entire life, eliminating the uncertainty of not knowing when you will die and whether your family is financially protected at the time of your death.

2. Includes a savings component designed to accumulate assets in a tax-efficient manner, which can be used for retirement supplementation, education funding, wedding expenses or any other way you want.

3. The term "Index" signifies that the savings component earns interest that is indirectly tied to the performance of a stock index. This potentially allows for a higher rate of return than traditional fixed rates, which allows assets to grow more rapidly and provides a hedge against inflation.

4. The term "Universal" stands for flexibility. You get to determine, within certain guidelines how much premium to pay, how often to pay premiums, to skip premiums altogether, how your assets are invested, when to take money out, how death benefits are payed and in some cases, you can even change the amount of insurance coverage.

Important Note:

While there will be some interchangeability of the terms, The Financial Pocketknife® concept represents more than Indexed Universal Life insurance by itself. It includes the choice of specific features and funding options identified in the book. The acronym IUL will be used for Indexed Universal Life Insurance throughout the book.

If a picture is worth a thousand words as the adage suggests, let's save a thousand and use this illustration for IUL:

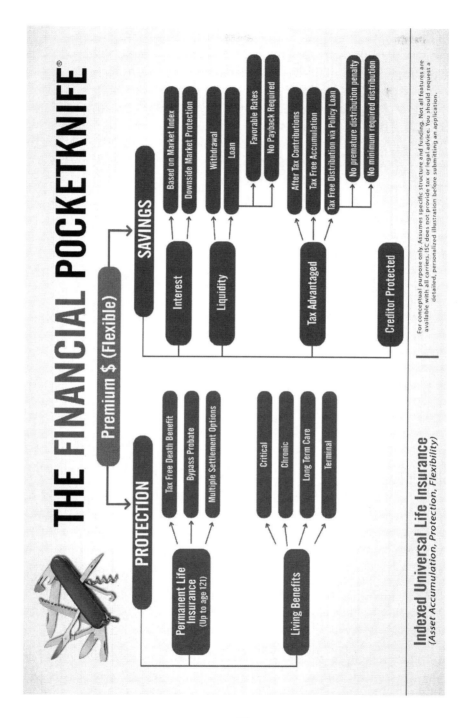

THE FINANCIAL POCKETKNIFE®

Premium $ (Flexible)

PROTECTION

Permanent Life Insurance (Up to age 121)
- Tax Free Death Benefit
- Bypass Probate
- Multiple Settlement Options

Living Benefits
- Critical
- Chronic
- Long Term Care
- Terminal

SAVINGS

Interest
- Based on Market Index
- Downside Market Protection

Liquidity
- Withdrawal
- Loan

- Favorable Rates
- No Payback Required

Tax Advantaged
- After Tax Contributions
- Tax Free Accumulation
- Tax Free Distribution via Policy Loan

- No premature distribution penalty
- No minimum required distribution

Creditor Protected

Indexed Universal Life Insurance
(Asset Accumulation, Protection, Flexibility)

For conceptual purpose only. Assumes specific structure and funding. Not all features are available with all carriers. ISC does not provide tax or legal advice. You should request a detailed, personalized illustration before submitting an application.

In reviewing the illustration, we want to visualize our Financial Pocketknife® as having two primary functions: protection and savings. Under each of these components, we will see the financial tools used to support each function.

For now, I just want you to use the illustration as a visual representation of IUL. As we go through the book, we will discuss all the underlying features (Living Benefits, Tax Advantaged, etc.) in greater detail, and you may want to refer to this picture to better assimilate the information. So, if you are one who likes to use book markers, this would be a good one to mark. You can also find a copy of the illustration on our website at www.thefinancialpocketknife.com.

There are, however, a few features that I want to highlight now that have an underlying impact on many of the benefits.

Policy Loans, The Secret Weapon

One of the first rules of science is if somebody delivers a secret weapon to you, you better use it.

Herbert Simon

Just as the lasso is Wonder Woman's secret weapon, the loan feature of IUL is the secret financial weapon that allows it (and other types of cash value policies) to be so powerful. While we will review the benefits of this feature in detail in the chapters to come, you should be aware that insurance companies are required by law to provide policyowner loans based on the policyowner's cash value (savings). You may be wondering why you would want to borrow your own money held by the insurance company much less why it would be considered a secret weapon. There are three primary reasons why borrowing money from your policy is incredibly valuable and why the loan feature is so critical to IUL.

First, it provides liquidity to the cash value of your policy. Unlike real estate or pension plans, your money is not locked up. You can access it at any time for any reason without qualification.

Second, IUL loans typically have a very low interest rate. In fact, many times you can effectively borrow at a rate of 0%, and in some scenarios, you can actually have a negative percentage effective rate. In other words, you can essentially take a loan that may provide a greater benefit than a 0% interest rate. Again, the conceptual and technical aspects will follow.

The last reason loans are so powerful, but not least important, is that proceeds from loans are not taxable. Because loans are not taxable, you are able to legally avoid paying taxes on all interest earned in your cash value.

And one more bombshell, you don't have to pay your life insurance loan back. Yes, you read it correctly: you don't have to pay your loan back!

If I don't have your complete attention at this point, go splash some water on your face and re-read this section again. This is powerful and exciting information that seems too good to be true but isn't. Wealthy people understand this tool, and you will too by the end of the book.

Flexibility

As stated earlier, IUL has great flexibility in terms of investment options, premium payments and benefits. In particular, the flexibility of premium payments is very favorable for the policy owner. Unlike traditional whole life or term policies, you can determine within certain parameters how much or how little to pay. The minimum amount you are required to pay is determined primarily by your age, health status, gender and face amount (the amount of life insurance). In some cases, you can skip premium payments altogether or pay an additional amount to increase your savings. Specifically, there are three levels of funding you need to be aware of: minimum, maximum, and target (or benchmark).

The "minimum" amount is the payment amount, based on insurance company assumptions, that must be allocated to the policy to keep it in force (active). Most companies today do not guarantee the minimum amount will keep the policy in force and reserve the right to change the minimum if their assumptions are not met. While this seems a little devious at first glance, this is rarely done for several reasons, including years of actuarial experience and client relations. The reality is that life insurance companies have suffered greatly over the past 20 years due to unprecedented periods of low interest rates and stock market volatility. These economic anomalies have prompted them to add "escape hatches" in their policies and reserve the right to raise the required premium if certain economic or company assumptions change due to unforeseen circumstances. Some companies, however, offer a "no-lapse guarantee" (NLG) that ensures a policy will stay in force if a specified premium is paid. There may be an additional charge for this guarantee, but it's an option to consider if you are highly risk averse.

The "maximum amount" of premium that can be placed in an IUL is restricted based on federal tax guidelines. Just like IRAs, 401(k)s and other types of retirement plans, the federal government limits the amount that can be put into an account because they don't want to forego tax revenues that would be lost if the amounts were unlimited. Unlike other retirement vehicles, however, the government does not have a set dollar amount for IUL plans (e.g., IRA limit = $5,500 per year).

Instead, the limit is restricted on a variable basis determined by different types of IRS guideline tests. While the details of these tests are beyond the scope of this writing, the basic concept is that the government outlines the definition of "life insurance" and takes the position that for a policy to receive favorable tax treatment, it must qualify under these definitions. Because of these tests, one could theoretically contribute $100,000 or more per year as long as their life insurance benefit is high enough to have the policy qualify as life insurance. Of course, individuals are limited to the amount of insurance they can purchase based on their income and assets so they, in effect, cannot contribute unlimited amounts.

There are three primary testing methods for IUL that are used to ensure that your policy does not lose its tax saving status: the 7-Pay test for modified endowment contracts (MECs), the Guideline Premium Test (GPT) and the Cash Value Accumulation Test (CVAT).

While the MEC test is mandatory for all policies, each policy either uses the GPT or the CVAT, but not both. Generally, the CVAT is reserved for traditional whole life policies, and the GPT is used for IUL. These IRS tests are very complicated and outside of the scope of this writing, but the main takeaway you should receive on this subject is that there is a maximum limit that you can contribute to your policy without causing negative tax consequences (loss of tax deferral on the returns and/or loss of tax-free exclusion on the death benefit for the beneficiary). You should seek tax guidance from a professional to see how these limits may affect you, if at all.

Since the CVAT is not normally used for IUL, only the GPT and MEC details are provided below.

Guideline Premium Test (GPT)
Under current federal tax law, the policy will qualify as life insurance only if: (a) the sum of premiums paid, less partial surrenders at any time, does not exceed the greater of the guideline single premium or the sum of the guideline level annual premiums at such time, and (b) the death benefit under the policy at any time is not less than the minimum required so that the policy falls within the cash value corridor as prescribed in section 7702(d) of the Internal Revenue Code.

Modified Endowment Contract (MEC)
The Technical and Miscellaneous Revenue Act of 1988 (TAMRA), which is effective for policies issued after June 21,1988, classifies certain policies as Modified Endowment Contracts (MEC). A life insurance policy becomes a MEC, as defined in section 7702A of the Internal Revenue Code, if at any time during the first seven policy years, the actual premiums paid exceeds the sum of an annually paid "7-Pay Premium."

If a policy violates the 7-Pay Premium test, it may be classified as a MEC retroactively to the time that it was issued. The 7-Pay Premium is the level annual premium that could fund all future benefits without regard to loads and expenses under the policy in seven years. All distributions, including loans, from a MEC may be taxable to the extent there is a gain in the policy. In addition, such distributions prior to age 59 ½ may be subject to an additional 10% penalty. Changes made at any time to a policy will affect the TAMRA 7-Pay Premium. Any material changes to the policy could result in the policy being reclassified as a MEC retroactively to its date of issue. Changes in the premium payments could also cause the policy to be classified as a MEC. You should ask the insurance company to recalculate the 7-Pay Premium before making any change to the policy.

It is extremely important that you do not contribute more funds to your policy than the limit amounts. Your financial professional will provide you with a hypothetical financial illustration that will list the dollar amount set by these limits. Additionally, your life insurance contract (policy) should also state this information.

Typically, the insurance company will monitor the GPT or CVAT limits closely on your behalf and should automatically restrict contributions that would violate the rule. However, you need to pay careful attention to your 7-Pay limit as there are cases when one may want to allow his or her policy to become a MEC, and the insurance company will not be as vigilant on your behalf.

Reference IRS Codes 7702 and 7702a MEC/7-Pay

Target premium (also known as benchmark premium) is the suggested premium to be paid on a level basis throughout the contract's duration to fund the policy so that it performs as designed to create a meaningful savings component and cover the insurance costs. Most clients AND agents don't realize that the target premium is only a suggestion made on behalf of the insurance company but is not required to be followed. As we discussed, only the minimum premium needs to be paid.

Note: The understanding of target premium is helpful when comparing policies of various companies. One company may have a lower target premium, which is normally how the premium is quoted, but that does not mean it is a less expensive or better performing policy. Rather, it may be more of a marketing and/or distribution strategy.

The obvious question is, "Why do insurance companies even use target premium if it is only a suggestion?" The answer is because the target premium is the amount that companies use to calculate and budget some of their internal expenses, including commission paid for distribution.

Further, it is typically used for policy illustrations to demonstrate how the policy should work. Last, it is much easier to communicate a target amount of premium to clients and agents than having to explain everything we just covered in this section.

Now that you know the different types of premiums, here is an example of how an illustration may look:

Planned Periodic Premium (max):	$276.02 Monthly
Monthly Guarantee Premium (min):	$63.05 Monthly
Target Premium:	$94.05 Monthly
Target Premium:	$1,128.60 Annually
Guideline Single Premium (GPT):	$15,756.43
Guideline Level Premium (GPT):	$3,312.39 Annually
7-Pay Premium (MEC):	$3,278.63 Annually

As we can see, if this were your policy, you would have the flexibility of paying as little as $63.05 per month (Monthly Guarantee Premium) or as much as $276.02 (Planned Periodic Premium). Of course, you can also annualize payments or skip some altogether as long as the minimum amount has been paid.

As a quick definitional note, "over-funding" refers to the amount of additional premium paid into a policy above the target amount, up to the maximum amount. You may see this term throughout the book, and it should not be confused with contributing more money to the policy than the IRS allows as previously explained in the above Nerd Alert.

Over-Funding/Max-Funding

Generally, most professionals will only suggest that you pay the target premium. The key to maximizing the results of an IUL, however, is to maximize the funding of your policy (max-fund). In other words, contribute as much money as you can into the policy without violating IRS guidelines. You may be thinking, "Of course the insurance company wants me to give them as much money as possible." But, it truly is to your benefit because it can lower your relative cost of the policy, build up your cash value (savings) more quickly, provide greater liquidity in the early years, and prevent the policy from lapsing (becoming inactive).

In terms of expenses, the more money you put into your policy, the lower your insurance cost as a percentage of premium becomes. Further, since several of your policy's expenses are calculated based on the amount of death benefit rather than premium, the policy expenses are also less costly relative to a higher contribution. In other words, you benefit from what economists call "economies of scale" when you put in more money. I know this may be on the verge of being categorized as a Nerd Alert, but the important thing to know conceptually is that when you put in more money, it works for you more efficiently because it has less "expense drag."

Because of adding more money and less expense drag, your cash value will build up more quickly than if you only contribute the target premium amount. This in turn, will lead to greater liquidity options in the early years as you will have access to your funds sooner because the cash available for withdrawals (or preferably a loan) will be greater than any amount "on hold" by the company to cover potential surrender charges. This concept may be confusing at this point in the book, but it should become clearer as we explain details in the chapters to come. At this point, just remember: more contributions equal greater liquidity in early years.

Last, when you over-fund or max-fund a policy, the chances of your policy lapsing (becoming inactive because of not being funded enough) become almost nil, ensuring that your permanent policy is truly permanent.

In my experience, if one is only paying the minimum to target on their policy, he or she is generally better served by reducing the death benefit of a policy so that he or she can max-fund the savings component and then supplement additional life coverage with a rider or convertible term. An important caveat is that first and foremost, you have to ensure that you have the appropriate amount of insurance to meet your needs.

Again, this material is a little advanced at this point of the book but necessary as a reference to discuss concepts in the following chapters. Just remember the premise for now, that it is to your benefit to contribute as much as you can into the policy. You may want to bookmark this page as a re-read if desired after you finish the book.

Accumulation Value vs. Cash Surrender Value

For definitional purposes, it is important to understand the difference between a policy's Accumulation Value and Cash Surrender Value. In most policies, you are subject to a Surrender Charge in the early years of the policy if you cancel it. This allows the insurance to recoup some of its expenses for underwriting and distributing the policy. The Cash Surrender Value is simply the difference between your Accumulation Value and your applicable Surrender Charge as defined by your policy. Once your Surrender Period is over (defined in your policy), the Accumulation Value and Cash Surrender Value become equal. Understanding this will be helpful when you review your personalized illustration and for later discussions in the book. Here are the technical definitions:

The Accumulation Value is the cash accumulation component of the policy. It reflects net premiums received, withdrawals made, expenses charged, cost of insurance deducted and interest credited. It is sometimes referred to as Cash Value.

The Cash Surrender Value is the amount available to the owner when the policy is terminated for a reason other than the Insured's death. This is equal to the Cash Value less policy loans and accumulated interest.

Long-Term Strategy

IUL is not a get-rich-quickly scheme or for someone with a short-term outlook. You should know and understand that many of the techniques and benefits discussed in this book are based on the scenario that you have a long-term outlook.

Checks and Dashes for Quadrants

In the chapters to come, we will break down the DKRQ into its four components and evaluate how the Financial Pocketknife® attacks each of the Dream Killers. As we go through each risk, we will assign one of three outcomes that you will see highlighted in the illustration. Providing the risk is eliminated or significantly mitigated, the risk will get a checkmark (✓). If the risk is not eliminated but positively impacted in some way, the risk will receive a partial checkmark in the form of a dash (–). Finally, if the Financial Pocketknife does not impact a risk, the box will be left empty.

Now that we understand the basics of the Financial Pocketknife, let's get started on beating the Dream Killers!

Chapter 5

QI, Protect This House!
(Physical Risks)

Anyone who does not provide for their relatives, and especially for their own household, has denied the faith and is worse than an unbeliever.

1 Timothy 5:8

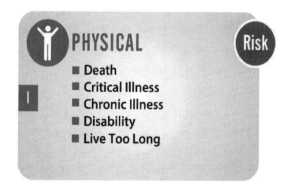

If you are a sports fan, you have surely observed pregame football rituals where the teams huddle together and get "psyched" to compete against their rivals. The home team often begins to yell at each other and scream loudly "Protect This House"! It is an emphatic statement that nobody comes into the team's home field, in front of their home fans and beats them! It's a reminder to players to sacrifice everything they have and play as hard as they can to make sure their house is protected.

Wouldn't it be great if we began our mornings like that every day as we take on the world? Perhaps we should collect our team (family) every day at home and chant "Protect This House"! We should all be resolute that nobody and nothing is going to invade our house and kill our dreams – that to the best of our ability, no matter what, we are going to do our best to protect each other and our dreams.

To help us with that, let's see how the Financial Pocketknife® applies to Quadrant I, Protection.

Death

First and foremost, above all, IUL serves as life insurance to protect your family against premature death. If you have people who depend on you financially and you don't have life insurance, you are flat out being irresponsible and selfish. This is a strong statement, sounds judgmental and will surely offend some readers, but I absolutely stand by it because it is the truth. I personally know the devastation of people acting this way because I have experienced it. When you see a family go through the premature loss of a loved one, it's heartbreaking. When you see this happen without life insurance, it is tragic!

For many companies, the term "permanent" means you are covered until age 121. Not only do you have lifetime protection, but death proceeds are paid to your beneficiaries income- tax-free and avoids probate court. Additionally, you can choose different settlement options. For example, instead of lump-sum payment, you can choose that payments are made monthly over a period of time.

Living Benefits (Long-Term Care, Chronic, Critical, Terminal)
The second form of protection that IUL provides is a relatively new feature in the industry called Living Benefits. Living Benefits are benefits that you don't have to die to use. Interestingly, this protection benefits YOU while you are still living rather than only being a benefit that your beneficiaries receive upon your death. Specifically, you may have options for chronic, critical, and terminal illness and/or long-term care in which you can receive part of your death benefit tax-free while you are living to help pay for medical bills, time off work, or any other reason. Not all companies offer these benefits and, for those companies that do, there is little

66

uniformity of how the benefits are offered and administered. Generally, these additional benefits are offered by the voluntary option of adding insurance riders to your policy. An insurance rider is an option offered to policyholders for an additional type of coverage separate from the primary coverage (in this case life coverage). Some riders are offered with no additional expense while others have a charge.

Chronic Illness

The great news is that Americans are living longer. Due to technological and medical advancements, there is a growing population of elderly. By 2030, it is projected that the number of individuals age 65 and older will be more than 71 million, almost twice the number today. The not so great news is that because of increased life expectancy, you will have a pretty good chance of experiencing a chronic illness that will require significant assets to treat. According to the U.S. Department of Health and Human Services, about 70% of individuals over the age of 65 will require some type of long-term care service during their lifetimes. Over 40% of all people will need care in a nursing home for some period.

Although companies may differ in their definition and coverage, typically a chronic illness is an illness or physical condition which permanently affects an individual so that he or she:

- Is unable to perform at least two of the six Activities of Daily Living (bathing, dressing, toileting, transferring, continence, eating) without substantial assistance; or

- Requires substantial supervision by another person to protect an individual from threats to health and safety due to severe cognitive impairment, and for which the individual is under a plan of care prescribed by a licensed health care practitioner.

Chronic Illness is a Dream Killer that few think about until they are exposed to it personally, either through personal health or that of a loved one, especially a parent. However, this Dream Killer can ruin families and is often misunderstood. There are several myths you should understand.

Myth #1 – Chronic Illness is something that young people don't need to worry about.

I already know what you are thinking! "Long-Term Care is for the elderly. It's an issue that I don't need to worry about until I am old, AFTER I have fulfilled all my dreams." Most people erroneously believe this idea and don't think about the need for long-term care until they get into their 60s. The reality, however, is that chronic illness does not discriminate based on age. An article written for a Georgetown University project on Long-Term Care Financing stated that nearly 43% of those who need long-term care are between the ages of 18 and 64. Younger people just don't think about chronic illness caused by accidents and health related events (e.g., congenital defect, stroke).

Overall, the risk of one needing long-term health care at some point in their life is a 50/50 proposition.

Myth #2 – Medical insurance covers long-term care.

Contrary to popular belief, health insurance (including Medicare) does not cover Long-Term Care. While it may cover some of the costs associated with an acute illness (cause of illness), it does not cover ongoing care.

Myth # 3 – I can always rely on Social Security/Medicaid if needed.

Social Security/Medicaid coverage can be very confusing and challenging in general, not to mention that each state has its own rules. There are a few commonalities that you should understand, however. First, many long-term facilities do not accept Medicaid. As a result, your options may be limited and, in many cases, you may not find a facility that is close to your home. More importantly, to qualify for Medicaid, you typically cannot have more than $2,000 in liquid assets. That's right, you read it correctly, $2,000 in liquid assets! And, if you think you will outsmart the system and transfer your assets to family members, you should be aware that you must do so five years BEFORE you apply. Last, Medicaid has an "Estate Recapture" provision which requires your estate to pay back the benefits you received from Medicaid upon your death. So, the proceeds from the sale of your home, car, and personal belongings get paid to Medicaid before they go to any of your heirs.

Myth # 4 – My family will take care of me.

While much of the care for those with chronic illness is provided by family members, the reality is that most family members already have other commitments (i.e., a job and family) that inhibit them from taking care of a chronically ill person. More importantly, they rarely possess the skill set needed to care for many of the challenges associated with chronic illness.

Myth # 5 – If I become chronically ill, I probably won't survive long anyway so I don't need to worry too much about resources.

According to the National Care Planning Council, the average stay in a nursing home is 835 days (2.5 years). Remember, that's the average, so you may be in a nursing home for a much longer period and need to plan accordingly.

I can't stress enough how important it is to protect yourself from Chronic Illness. You can spend a lifetime sacrificing and saving, just to lose it all from a chronic illness and/or strain the resources of your family members. It is common for adult children to find themselves in the position of having to help aging parents financially when they become affected by a chronic illness. And, guess when it often happens? If you guessed the same time that the adult child has children of their own in college (perhaps the most expensive time of a parent's life), you would be correct. So, if you are in this situation (commonly referred to as the "sandwich generation"), you get to choose whether to help your parents (and protect your potential inheritance) or help your child. This is a great reason to help your parents plan for this potential scenario and purchase insurance BEFORE they need it.

Another important factor to consider is what happens to a surviving spouse once one enters long-term care and, presumably passes away first. Because of the tremendous cost associated with long-term care, the surviving spouse often finds herself in financial strain and struggles greatly as a widow(er).

Fortunately, IUL can help protect you against Chronic Illness. Functionally, it does so by providing two types of insurance riders; a Chronic Illness rider or a Long-Term Care rider. As stated, each company that offers chronic illness protection, does so in their own individual way so it is important that you read the details of the rider and work with a professional who understands the little nuances of each.

Note: not all companies offer Chronic Illness coverage on their products and the coverage is state specific. So, while the company's brochure may highlight the coverage, it may not be available in your state. You may also find that due to the maximum benefit payouts provided by the chronic illness/LTC protection of a life insurance policy (which are based on your chosen death benefit), that additional coverage is needed.

Chronic Illness Rider vs Long-Term Care

Long-term care (LTC) and chronic illness riders are similar in many ways, especially in terms of qualification for benefits. There are some significant differences, however. In particular, there are differences on how the benefits are calculated, the type of documentation needed for a claim and how frequently it has to be submitted, whether or not receipts are required, the maximum amount of monthly and lifetime benefits, how the death benefit is impacted upon a claim, the type of payment (reimbursement vs indemnity), and who can actually provide the care.

Life insurance companies normally offer one type of coverage or the other, if at all. Because of the multitude of options and complexity of Chronic Illness vs LTC, I could literally write a whole book on the subject but that is not the purpose of this book. For a consumer, my best advice is to work with a professional who can help you chose the right policy for your individual needs and goals. As you will see in the chapters to come, I am a big advocate of professional advice and discuss in detail the merits of using one in *Chapter 12 – Putting it All Together.*

Critical Illness

It is very important that you review the coverage listed by the company offering the coverage, but depending on the company, critical illness generally includes major heart attack, coronary artery bypass, stroke, invasive cancer, blood cancers (leukemia, lymphoma, multiple myeloma), major organ transplant, end stage renal failure, paralysis, coma and severe burn. Think about the significance of this benefit. I have a family member who had quintuple bypass heart surgery over twenty years ago and is healthy as a horse today. If you develop a critical illness, how comforting will it be to know that you have the financial option to utilize your life insurance if needed for medical expenses, family needs, or any other reason? And, you won't have to deplete your retirement account as a result and can enjoy years of health to come.

Terminal Illness

Terminal illness is an illness or physical condition that is certified by a licensed physician to be reasonably expected to result in an individual's death within 24 months from the date of certification. With IUL, if you are diagnosed with a terminal illness, you can withdrawal funds based on your death benefit tax free. Notice, I stated death benefit not cash value! This means you have access to a much greater amount. Of course, whatever amount you withdraw will reduce the death benefit provided to your beneficiaries after your death.

Disability

Let me state emphatically that IUL is not a disability policy. In recent years, some companies have made progress in adding disability elements to their policies as riders, but we don't yet have a true disability feature for IUL. Unfortunately, some advisors market the Chronic and Critical Illness features of an IUL as disability protection, but these features do not provide traditional disability coverage and agents should not imply such.

Disability is an important coverage that is often overlooked, but you have a much greater chance of becoming disabled than dying prematurely as we learned in Chapter 2. While I am not an advocate of workplace life insurance, I do believe there is value in workplace disability insurance. Either way, Disability is a Dream Killer that you need to protect yourself from.

Live Too Long

The idea of Living Too Long being a Dream Killer may sound humorous at first thought. It sounds like an oxymoron, similar to jumbo shrimp. After all, isn't it everyone's goal to live as long as possible? The concept of living too long doesn't necessarily apply to our physical life but more to the idea of outliving our assets, which is arguably a bigger challenge now than ever.

People are surprised to learn that the average life expectancy 100 years ago was only 53. They are even more surprised to learn that Social Security was never meant to be a retirement plan as it is viewed by many today but rather to be insurance for those elderly citizens who were desolate and could no longer work. In fact, while the benefit age was originally set at 65 at the time of its inception, life expectancy was only 61.7. That's right: the average person died before they received benefits.

Today, people are living much longer due to medical and technology advancements, and the average life expectancy is almost 79 and one can spend 20 to 30 years in retirement.

Because IUL offers a very effective supplement to one's retirement plan by creating cash value, having favorable investment options, and tax free liquidity, the Dream Killer of Living Too Long can be minimized by The Financial Pocketknife but does not offer full protection unless funded properly to meet all retirement needs. As such, it receives a partial check in our DKRQ.

QI Conclusion

The Financial Pocketknife® has many effective tools to combat Physical Risks. It protects against Death, Critical Illness and Chronic Illness and can assist as a supplementary fund to guard against Living Too Long. While the cash value can help with expenses during a Disability, it does not offer protection against long-term disability.

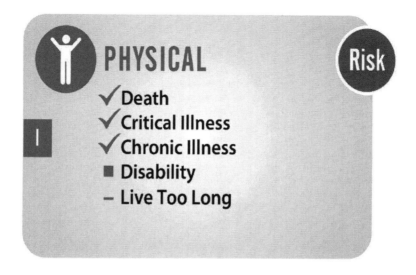

Chapter 6
QII, Offense AND Defense (Financial Risks)

You have to develop your whole game to completion.

Isaiah Thomas

In sports, there is constant debate on the importance of offense versus defense. Football, in particular, is a sport where coaches (and teams) are known for being either offensive-minded OR defensive-minded. While one team may have a lot of resources invested in their offense and score a lot of points, they fail to win championships because they ignore their defense and give up even more points to their opponents than they score. Likewise, teams who focus on defense often keep their opponents from scoring but struggle with scoring themselves.

Championship teams, however, understand that you must have a great offense AND a great defense. You cannot sacrifice one at the expense of the other.

Similarly, to be a champion in the money game you must have the same balance of offense and defense.

Champions have a great offense AND a great defense!

In the last chapter we spoke about "protecting our house" with an emphasis on defense. In this chapter, we will continue to learn about defensive tactics for Financial Dream Killers but also explore the need for offense in some scenarios.

Inflation Risk

One of the biggest needs for offense is to beat inflation. Inflation is a hidden risk that is often overlooked and misunderstood by people. Historically, inflation has risen an average of 3-4% each year. However, many people believe the rate is typically higher than government reports due to the manipulation of key government indicators. For instance, the U.S. government removed the cost of energy and food from their calculation of inflation (CPI) in the 1990s under the guise that the two categories are too volatile for consistent tracking. Of course, we still need food and energy in times of inflation. The reality is that they just don't want the public to see a high inflation number because it can psychologically have a negative impact on consumers, cause markets to decline, and lead to economic problems (and political criticism).

Some categories of goods and services certainly rise at a higher rate than the norm. For instance, planners are normally taught to include an 8% annual rise in inflation for college tuition. And, as most of us already know, healthcare and health insurance have skyrocketed over the past 20 years.

Regardless of which data you use, one very important mathematical theorem remains constant.

If you don't earn an amount of interest on your savings account equal to, or more than, the rate of inflation, you are losing money (purchasing power).

Let's use an example for simplicity. Say that you made a deal with your daughter when she went to college that if she graduated in four years, you will buy her a $10,000 car. To motivate her, you deposit $10,000 into a CD at your bank that is currently paying 1%. Your daughter excels in college and graduates right at the four-year mark. Your account has grown to a whopping $10,406. Hold on though; before we cash out, we still have to pay taxes on the earnings. After taxes, the account drops to $10,345 (15% simple tax for illustrative purposes). We are now ready to go buy that car.

But wait, the car no longer costs $10,000 due to inflation but is now listed at $11,699 (at 4% annual inflation). You are $1,354 dollars short because the interest return on your CD did not keep up with inflation. You not only have to come up with the difference to pay for the car, but if you think about, you even have to earn more than $1,354 because of income taxes. Depending on your tax bracket, you may need to earn an additional $500 dollars or more.

The consumer psychology of loss and inflation is quite fascinating. As humans, most of us tend to have a mindset that is focused on what we already "have in hand" and not so much on what we may be giving up. We don't want to take the risk of losing what we already have, despite the fact that we may be able to get much more if we refocus on what we may be missing out on if we don't take advantage of an opportunity. Economists refer to this as "opportunity cost." Think about our CD scenario.

What if the bank sent you a letter that it had been robbed, and as a result, your portion of the robbery equaled $1,354? Due to this loss, your CD is now only worth $8,646 ($10,000 - $1,354). If you are like me, I imagine you would be outraged at this news. Without hesitation, you would be on the phone calling the bank manager and may say a couple of choice words. Yet, when inflation steals our $1,354, we don't even realize it. Or, we justify it in our mind by thinking that the

CD investment was worth the low return because we avoided a possible loss in the stock market. In the end, however, regardless of how the money disappeared, we are still out of the same amount. Shouldn't we be just as outraged regardless of how it was lost?

On a larger scale, when we consider larger amounts of savings over a longer period of time, we can literally lose hundreds of thousands of dollars due to inflation.

Unfortunately, we face risk no mater how we invest our money. If we put our funds in a CD, we lose to inflation, and if we put it in the market, we may lose to market risk.

The great news, however, is that with money in an IUL policy, we can get the best of both worlds. We can mitigate both inflation and market risk. To stick with our analogy, we can have a great offense (indexed interest) to fight inflation and a great defense (guaranteed floor interest rate) to protect against market risk.

Perhaps the most unique benefit of an IUL is the indexed interest option which allows you to receive a stock market-based return with guaranteed downside market protection. While the mechanics of this feature are very technical, the basic thing to understand is that you receive a return on the savings portion of your account based on a stock market index, but you are guaranteed to never lose money if the market goes down.

Because Market Risk and Inflation Risk are inversely tied together, more details on how the Financial Pocketknife® fights them simultaneously will be highlighted in the Market Risk section next. But for now, understand that the Dream Killer of Inflation is mitigated due to the Indexed Option feature of IUL, and therefore, our DKRQ gets a check mark.

Market Risk

Indexed Interest

One of the great savings challenges that society has is how to maximize returns while reducing the risk of market loss and/or volatility. Perhaps the most innovative feature in the industry in many years is how interest is credited in an IUL. Interest in an IUL is credited based on a stock market index, but the insurance company guarantees that your account will never lose money if the stock market loses money.

This technique allows you to have indirect stock market returns for potentially higher rates of return than traditional savings accounts but eliminates your downside risk. For example, if the market goes down 20% or 30% during a defined period of time, the insurance company will guarantee your account stays at 0% return, or in some cases, actually receives a nominal return. Alternatively, if the stock market goes up, your account will receive an interest credit based on a chosen stock market index.

This seems too good to be true, doesn't it? How can a company allow for such upside potential but guarantee no loss? The answer is that there IS a catch. In order for the company to provide a guarantee on downside protection, they must limit the upside gain.

Based on current practices today, companies will cap the upside between 11 and 14%. This means that if the market goes up by 20% or 30%, your account would be capped at 14%. So effectively, you are guaranteed to receive an interest rate of between 0% and 14% in our example.

This is an incredibly important feature because mathematically it is more important NOT TO have a negative return than have a positive return. For example, if you were to lose 50% on an account, most people don't understand that you would have to receive a 100% return (not a 50%) return just to get back to your original balance. (See Chapter 3, *Wax On, Wax Off*, for a refresher if needed.)

Indexes

An index is a statistical measure of change in an economy or a securities market. In the case of financial markets, an index is an imaginary portfolio of securities representing a particular market or a portion of it. (Investopedia)

Over the last 15 years, 92.2% of large-cap funds lagged a simple S&P 500 index fund. The percentages of mid-cap and small-cap funds lagging their benchmarks were even higher: 95.4% and 93.2%, respectively.

Standard and Poor's Research, Market Watch 2017

When you allocate your payments into an "indexed" account within an IUL policy, it's important to understand that your funds are not directly invested into an index. Rather, the insurance company credits your account interest payments based on the performance of a specified index. The insurance company is managing the money in its general account, and you have no direct ownership in the index funds they use.

Index Cap and Participation Rate Index

As previously stated, in order for insurance companies to guarantee that stock market linked interest accounts will not have negative returns, they must place limits on the amount of upside earnings for the policies to work actuarily. Without these upside limits, the insurance company would have to substantially increase the policy charges at the consumer's detriment. These "ceilings" are stated in your illustration but are subject to change up or down at the company's discretion and market conditions. There are two primary methods insurance companies use to limit the return on index interest, the Cap Rate and Participation Rate.

The Cap Rate method simply limits the upside earnings based on a percentage of return. For example, a 12% cap would limit the annual earning rate to 12%. So, if the stock market index grew by 20% in a given period of time, the policy owner would only receive 12% interest, not a 20% return.

Instead of limiting the upside earnings based on a defined percentage, the Participation Rate limits the earnings based on a percentage of the market's earnings rate. For example, if a Participation Rate is set at 70%, the policy owner would receive 70% of the stock market index return. So, if the stock market index return was 20%, the policy owner would receive a return of 14% (70% of 20%).

Different companies offer different cap methods, but it is not uncommon for a company to offer both methods. You get to choose which interest account you allocate your contributions to and may also have the option of splitting your allocation into both account types.

🤓 **Nerd Alert!**

Here is an example of a hypothetical account for illustrative purposes:

Historical Index Changes and Hypothetical Interest Rates
The table below shows the actual historical index changes and the corresponding hypothetical interest rates for each Index Account for the most recent 20-year period, assuming that the index parameters each year are the same as the current values for these parameters:

Current Index Cap for Index Cap Account: 11.00%
Current Participation Rate for Participation Rate Account: 70.00%

The table below reflects the actual historical 1-year point-to-point returns of the S&P 500 for the Index Cap Account and the Participation Rate Account from Dec. 31, 1995, to Dec. 31, 2015. It also reflects the hypothetical annualized current non-guaranteed index parameters for the 1-Year Index. Accounts could be over the same period. Past performance is not indicative of future performance.

Actual performance may vary, perhaps materially, from the performance set forth herein.

		Index Cap Account 1-Year Point-to-Point S&P Index 500®		Participation Rate Account 1-Year Point-to-Point S&P 500®	
Begin Date	End Date	Index Growth Rate	Index Growth Rate	Index Growth Rate	Hypothetical Interest Credited
12/31/1995	12/31/1996	20.26%	11.00%	20.26%	14.18%
12/31/1996	12/31/1997	31.01%	11.00%	31.01%	21.71%
12/31/1997	12/31/1998	26.67%	11.00%	26.67%	18.67%
12/31/1998	12/31/1999	19.53%	11.00%	19.53%	13.67%
12/31/1999	12/31/2000	-10.14%	0.25%	-10.14%	0.25%
12/31/2000	12/31/2001	-13.04%	0.25%	-13.04%	0.25%
12/31/2001	12/31/2002	-23.37%	0.25%	-23.37%	0.25%
12/31/2002	12/31/2003	26.38%	11.00%	26.38%	18.47%
12/31/2003	12/31/2004	8.99%	8.99%	8.99%	6.30%
12/31/2004	12/31/2005	3.00%	3.00%	3.00%	2.10%
12/31/2005	12/31/2006	13.62%	11.00%	13.62%	9.53%
12/31/2006	12/31/2007	3.53%	3.53%	3.53%	2.47%
12/31/2007	12/31/2008	-38.49%	0.25%	-38.49%	0.25%
12/31/2008	12/31/2009	23.45%	11.00%	23.45%	16.42%
12/31/2009	12/31/2010	12.78%	11.00%	12.78%	8.95%
12/31/2010	12/31/2011	0.00%	0.25%	0.00%	0.25%
12/31/2011	12/31/2012	13.41%	11.00%	13.41%	9.38%
12/31/2012	12/31/2013	29.60%	11.00%	29.60%	20.72%
12/31/2013	12/31/2014	11.39%	11.00%	11.39%	7.97%
12/31/2014	12/31/2015	-0.73%	0.25%	-0.73%	0.25%
Compound Annual Average			6.79%		8.34%

Note: It is important to understand that your funds are not directly invested in the stock market or the indexes. Instead, the insurance company credits your account interest based on the performance of a chosen index. Insurance companies need to share this information with you for legal and regulatory purposes, but it normally just causes more confusion for all involved. For conceptual purposes, you just need

82

to understand that your interest credits are directly correlated with the chosen market indexes and are credited in a substantially similar manner.

Because of the downside protection guaranteed by IUL, the Dream Killer of Market Risk earns a full check mark.

Tax Risk

The only difference between death and taxes is that death doesn't get worse every time Congress meets.

Will Rogers

How many of us voluntarily send in extra money to the government with our tax returns? The answer is none, zero, zilch! I've never met one person who decided to make a charitable contribution to the IRS. As the CEO of my family, I have a responsibility to maximize my advantages within the guidelines of the law. Yet, many people involuntarily make charitable contributions to the IRS by not understanding the tax laws or taking advantage of opportunities to save money from taxes.

Most of us are familiar with the tax advantages of IRAs and 401(k)s, where you get a tax deduction for investing and tax deferral on earnings but have to pay taxes on ALL the proceeds upon the withdrawal. The question one has to ask is, "Why we would want to pay taxes on the harvest instead of the seed?" In other words, there are times when it may be more advantageous to pay for taxes upfront and never again on the accumulation and distribution.

You do not get a tax deduction for your contributions into an IUL policy. But, since internal earnings are tax deferred in life insurance policies and you can take loans which never have to be paid back on your IUL policy, you are able to legally avoid paying taxes on any earnings you receive on your internal savings account. You simply continue to take loans out of your policy until you pass away. And at the time of your death, your death benefit will pay off your loan, and the rest is paid to your beneficiaries tax-free! The effective result of this technique is that your accumulated earnings never get taxed!

Note: Refer to Chapter 4, *The Financial Pocketknife®*, as a refresher on how loans work, if needed.

🤓 Nerd Alert!

Income Tax – How High can it Go?

The old adage "Give an inch, and they take a mile!" could not apply better when it comes to the U.S. government. Most people are surprised to learn that for the first 137 years of the U.S., there was no income tax. Yes, you heard it correctly: there was no income tax.

The idea of an income tax came into play in the early 1900s as a way to finance World War I. To legalize it, the federal government had to create a constitutional amendment and sold it to the public by promoting the idea that it would be applied only to the wealthy and was set at a mere 2%. Of course, once the politicians got their foot in the door, the rates continually went higher and higher to an all-time marginal rate of ... ready for it? ... 92%!!!! Yes, 92%!!!!

The **Sixteenth Amendment (Amendment XVI)** to the United States Constitution allows Congress to levy an income tax without apportioning it among the states or basing it on the United States Census. This amendment exempted income taxes from the constitutional requirements regarding direct taxes, after income taxes on rents, dividends and interest were ruled to be direct taxes in the court case of *Pollock v. Farmers' Loan & Trust Co.* (1895). The amendment was adopted on February 3, 1913. (Wikipedia*)*

One major issue to consider is the overall top marginal tax rates. In the illustration below, you can see the top marginal income tax rates dating back to 1913. From 1933 through 1982, the top marginal tax rates were above 60%. After that point they reduced to near-historic lows, where they've held pretty constant ever since.

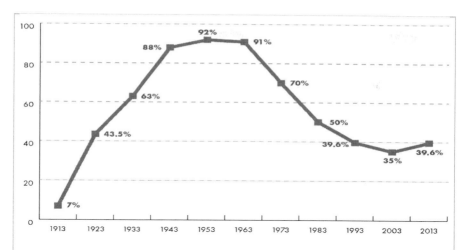

But what about future income tax rates? Many people theorize that with today's challenging economic issues (constant deficits, public debt, solvency of entitlement programs), tax rates will go up once again in the future. If true, the importance of IUL as a protection against taxes becomes even greater! Imagine taking distributions from your 401(k) as a retiree just to find that the government taxes it at an exorbitant rate. Doesn't it make sense to pay taxes at the current historical low rate than to possibly be subject to additional taxes based on the government's mismanagement of the country's finances?

As we learned earlier in the book, by taking distributions from an IUL through the loan option, you never pay taxes on your accumulated funds. As a result, you don't need to worry about future income tax rates no matter how high they climb (even if they go back to 92%). Further, you are not subject to a premature distribution tax penalty for taking money out before you are 59 ½ years old. So if you ever need to access cash values because you are out of work, want to start a business, or pay for college or a wedding, not only do you not have to pay income tax, but you also don't have a tax penalty. Remember, these tax benefits only apply if you take the money out in the form of a loan.

If you take money out as a withdrawal (not in the form of a loan), you still have some tax advantages in that your money has grown tax-deferred, you get to use a favorable cost basis because you can include the cost of insurance, and you generally are taxed on the FIFO method (First In, First Out); but you are still subject to income tax and a premature penalty if you are under 59 ½.

Last, you are not subject to minimum required distributions when you reach 70 ½ years of age as you are with traditional retirement plans. This helps protect you from taxes in your retirement years, especially since we can't predict what taxes will be in the future.

It is important to know that you must keep your policy in-force (active) to benefit from this tax technique. If a policy lapses, there can be significant tax consequences. We do not offer tax advice, and you should seek appropriate professional help as needed.

🤓 Nerd Alert!

IRC Codes and Disclaimers
Death benefits paid to the beneficiary are free of income tax (IRC 101(a)(1)). Increments in the cash surrender value are not includible in the taxable income of the policy owner (IRC 72(e))

Proceeds from a life insurance policy are generally income-tax-free and if properly structured, may also be free from estate tax.

Income-tax-free distributions are achieved by withdrawing to the cost basis (premiums paid) then using policy loans. Policy loans and withdrawals may generate an income-tax liability, reduce available cash value and reduce the death benefit or cause the policy to lapse.

This material is provided for general and educational purposes only; it is not intended to provide legal, tax or investment advice. All investments are subject to risk. We recommend that you consult an independent legal or financial advisor for specific advice about your individual situation.

The information herein is not intended to be used, and cannot be used by any taxpayer, for the purpose of avoiding tax penalties. Taxpayers should seek advice based on their own particular circumstances from an independent tax advisor.

Liquidity

I have worked with retired couples who had plenty of assets in real estate and were forced to sell their homes because they lacked liquid assets. They did not have access to the cash in their homes to pay for unforeseen circumstances when needed. While paying off a home is a common goal for most people, a very valid argument can be made that it is not the best use of money. I could write a whole chapter on the argument based on several perspectives, but that's not in the realm of this book. The important consideration for our current purpose is to understand that the ability to have access to your assets is very important.

Liquidity is an important aspect of any financial plan. Assuming your IUL is properly structured and funded, you are able to access your account through withdrawals, but also have an opportunity to access funds through a favorable loan to yourself. This loan feature is specific to life insurance and a special provision listed in the IRS tax code that is not very well known by most people.

Specifically, you are able to borrow money from your own account at a specified rate (let's say 6%) but get credited back a similar rate on your own money (let's say 6% for the credit rate, too). So effectively, you were able to access your money for 0%. In some cases, believe it or not, if your savings account earns more than 6%, your loan rate figuratively becomes negative. Think about that last statement. If you borrow money at 6% and still have money in your saving account earning a higher rate (let's say 8%), can't we make the argument that your real cost of money is -2% (6% - 8%)?

If that feature seems incredible by itself, there is even better news: you are NOT required to pay back the loan. Again, you are NOT required to pay back the loan. Zero! Since your account is secured by your own money and the insurance company is not relying on your loan for its profitability, you are not required to pay back the loan.

You are probably asking yourself, "Why would the insurance company lend money out, not charge a large interest rate, and not require me to pay the loan back?" There are several answers to this question. First, insurance companies are required by law to make loans to their policyowners based on the policy's cash value. Second, insurance companies profit from other sources including the cost of insurance, expense charges and investment returns. They do not typically rely on loan interest as a profit driver, although they normally assess a fee to cover processing expenses. Third, as we pointed out earlier, the ability to use loans to avoid taxes is a key competitive advantage of life insurance. Without this advantage, life insurance companies understand their sales would significantly decline. Finally, since loans are secured by a policy's cash value, there is little to no risk of the insurance company losing money when a loan is not paid back.

Note: It is important to understand that each company has its own policy regarding loans. Some companies do charge a spread for loans, and most companies charge an administrative fee. Read your illustration and policy for details.

Debt

The term Debt in the context of a Dream Killer doesn't necessarily apply to all debt but rather bad debt. Yes, that means there are such things as good debt. There is a prevalent thought and practice among many in society that they should strive to be debt-free. While this is a noble thought and practice, it doesn't always hold true from a technical perspective. Being debt-free may make us feel better emotionally but can also hinder us financially.

If you look at the largest companies in the world, they all issue debt despite having billions of dollars of cash in their coffers. Apple Inc., the largest company in the world by market value, at the time of this writing has almost $242 billion in debt despite being very profitable. Why would such large companies use debt if they have so much cash and are so profitable? The answer is for the same reason that you see a bank name displayed at the top of prominent buildings in most cities with a developed downtown: leverage. Per Investopedia, "leverage" is an investment strategy of using borrowed money – specifically, the use of various financial instruments or borrowed capital to increase the potential return of an investment.

Banks and businesses understand this concept of leverage and use it to maximize profits. Doesn't it then make sense that this same concept would be employed in our personal financial plan?

From a technical perspective, the answer is yes. However, most people misapply this concept and end up in serious trouble. There are four factors to consider when using debt in a personal plan.

First, debt should ideally be used to finance other assets that either retain value or have a likelihood of increasing in value. For instance, purchasing a home would meet this criterion, while taking a weekend excursion to Mexico would not.

Second, debt should not be excessive to the point that you cannot reasonably make the required payments. This is where most people get in trouble. They acquire much more debt than they can absorb from a cashflow perspective. Hence, the statistics we have cited on the U.S. debt and savings crisis. By the way, your debt ratios should be much lower than the guidelines required by lenders. Just because your bank approves you to borrow a bunch of money based on your credit report and financial picture doesn't mean you should.

Third, the key to leverage working in your favor is determined by the cost of money that you are borrowing versus the expected rate of return on the investment you are funding. If you can borrow money at a low percentage rate, let's say 6% for illustration purposes, and receive a return on your investment at a rate higher than 6%, you are technically better off because you receive the difference between the two rates. This is the reason why large companies borrow funds and banks make money.

Last and most important, the main determinant of whether debt is good is based on your ability to be self-disciplined. This is an area where we all have to be very honest with ourselves because most us don't have great self-discipline. If you are a person who can use debt as a form of leverage and not for spending sprees, then you may be able to use good debt for great benefit. If not, definitely strive to be debt-free and not acquire debt in the first place. Ironically, if you do not have self-discipline, you probably won't be able to do either option successfully.

If the definition of "bad debt" isn't obvious from these points, let's be clear that high-interest credit card debt used for perishable goods is a very bad use of debt, just as financing a brand new, overly high-priced car that depreciates significantly the moment you drive it off the lot would be.

This understanding of good and bad debt leads us to how IUL can help us with debt. Recall from Chapter 3, *The Financial Pocketknife®*, we discussed that the secret weapon of IUL was the feature of policy loans. We discussed that, providing you have built up enough cash value, you are able to borrow money from your policy at any time for any reason without qualification. We further discussed how interest was typically charged at a very low rate and offset by your cash value earnings. Last, we learned that you are not required to pay back your loan. If I am blowing your mind with these facts, you may want to go back and re-read the end of that chapter.

With this in mind, wouldn't it make much more sense to borrow from your policy than it would from a bank?

Think about this idea. A bank borrows funds at a low rate (e.g., 1%, the rate they pay you interest on your savings account) and lend that money back to you via your mortgage or credit card (up to 18%). They keep the difference of 17% (18% credit card revenue – 1% savings account interest paid). No wonder they can afford to put their name on all the big downtown buildings.

The math is pretty simple, under most circumstances: you are much better off borrowing from your insurance policy based on your own assets than you are from a bank. Further, remember that although it is to your benefit, you are not required to pay back your policy loan, which can significantly assist with the cash flow issue we discussed.

In addition to the loan option, the most powerful feature of IUL is, of course, that it is life insurance and provides a death benefit to your family when you pass away. This death benefit, if calculated correctly, should provide enough value to eliminate your family's debt obligations.

Because of this loan feature and death benefit, the Financial Pocketknife® can greatly impact or eliminate the Debt Dream Killer. However, because it cannot force you to have self-discipline and/or avoid excessive debt, it only receives a half checkmark in our Financial Quadrant.

Cash Flow

Cash Flow, as we defined it in Chapter 2, has a focus on personal income and expenses. The difference between these two factors, of course, equals the amount of money we have for saving – which, in turn, is the key driver for battling all of our Dream Killers.

At some point, most of us have had "too much month at the end of our check" where we have had to struggle to meet all of our monthly obligations. I used to play a game in college where my friends and I would go to the ATM to see who had the lowest balance. The highest balance got to pay for 39-cent tacos at Taco Bell. While I was excited that my low balance of 19 cents once won me a Taco Bell dinner, it is not fun as an adult to struggle with such issues. Unfortunately, I see this challenge a lot as a financial planner.

Long term, we have to follow a budget, make additional income, and/or minimize expenses to win the cash flow game. But in the short term, it is extremely helpful to have some flexibility in our expenses if needed. Although premium payments to an IUL represent savings and expenses, there is great flexibility in the amount that needs to be allocated each month to a policy, which tremendously helps with Cash Flow. As you may recall from Chapter 4, *The Financial Pocketknife®*, you only need to make a minimum payment to your policy to keep it active. And, if you have built up your cash value sufficiently, you can skip payments altogether. This is an extremely beneficial feature for those with variable income but also good for times when a little extra funds are required to meet unbudgeted expenses or emergency issues.

Because of the flexibility of payments for IUL, Cash Flow receives a partial check in our DKRQ. As much as we would like to believe that a product can solve this issue, winning the Cash Flow game ultimately comes down to your ability to produce income and manage expenses.

A Word about Variable Universal Life Insurance

Variable Universal Life Insurance (VUL) is the industry's predecessor to IUL. VUL typically offers the same benefits of IUL but is differentiated based on the savings component. Instead of your cash value account being tied to indexes, VUL offers a mutual fund-like investment option called a separate account. These investment options are not technically mutual funds, but in reality, they act the same way. In these accounts, you may choose many types of funds to invest in that are managed by professional money managers.

The upside to VUL is that you have more options from an investment perspective and are not limited by caps on market returns. The downside is that professional money managers rarely outperform indexes over a long period of time and VUL does not have guaranteed downside protection that IUL offers if the stock market tanks. While I am a bigger proponent of IUL because of this feature, I believe that VUL is a great product for those who have a higher risk tolerance and who believe in active management. You do need to be careful with these products if the market goes down dramatically because it not only impacts your account balance but may put your policy in jeopardy of lapsing if additional funding (premium) isn't added to compensate for market loss. In short, a VUL could be considered a Financial Pocketknife, but just one with less blades.

QII Conclusion

From a financial risk perspective, the Financial Pocketknife® is highly effective in beating the Dream Killers by providing protection against Inflation, Market Risk, Taxes and Liquidity Risk while giving Debt and Cashflow a good fight.

Chapter 7
QIII, The Serenity Prayer
(Environmental Risks)

God grant me the serenity to accept the things I cannot change;
courage to change the things I can; and wisdom to know the difference.

Reinhold Niebuhr

A common prayer in the Christian faith is the "Serenity Prayer." It helps us recognize that as much as we like to be in control, there are just some things that we don't have control over. Not being in control may mean that we can't prevent it from happening; however, we can attempt to manage and mitigate its consequence. For example, we can't control hurricanes hitting our home, but we can put up storm shutters, remove items that can fly around, make sure we buy a house on high ground, etc. (Can you tell I'm a Floridian?) While we can say that this concept applies to almost all our Dream Killers, in the Environmental Risk Quadrant we are referring to those risks in our external environment which are triggered by people and/or events other than yourself. While outside our span of control, these events can have a devastating impact.

One note if it isn't already obvious, by "Environmental" risk we are not referring to the ocean and trees; rather, we are referring to those things in life that can happen through no control of our own.

Quadrant III – Environmental Risks

In the Environmental Risk Quadrant, we see four general risks that can be Dream Killers. Each of these risks can have variations based on circumstances. For example, Job Loss could be due to one being fired or being laid off. Both of these circumstances are reasons for job loss but may be managed differently. This is an important distinction as we evaluate our method of mitigation and determine if IUL can help.

Life Emergency

By definition, life emergencies are urgent and unforeseen issues that disrupt our daily routine. The magnitude of these events can vary greatly and we could technically consider some of our other Dream Killers life emergencies (e.g., a critical illness). However, for our purposes, we consider Life Emergencies to be smaller in nature. Things such as a broken tooth, blown tire, paying for an insurance deductible or a pet's torn ACL repair. These are events we never think about or imagine occurring, but as luck would have it, happen to all of us at times.

While these risks are not ones that typically cause bankruptcy, they can often lead to larger expenses and have a spiraling effect leading to a much larger cost. For instance, perhaps you ignore a small mechanical issue in your car due to lack of funds, and that issue, in turn, causes your car's engine to blow up entirely, rendering it useless. As the saying goes, small holes sink big ships!

One of three pillars of financial planning is to have an emergency fund for these life emergencies. The specific amount will vary based on your circumstances, but typically a threshold of $1,000 is a good goal to set for our emergency fund. This is the amount for most of the population that would cause some pain if it were to be needed unexpectedly.

According to a 2017 GOBankingRates survey, more than half of Americans (57%) have less than $1,000 in their savings accounts.

The dollars set aside for your emergency fund should have two requirements. The first is that it is liquid, and the second is that it will not be subject to any type of investment loss.

Because of these requirements, most people just put their emergency money into a bank savings account. While such an account certainly meets the requirement of an emergency fund, the downside is that it pays little to no interest and the money can sometimes be "too liquid" in that it can tempt one to stretch the definition of emergency. No, buying a new 70-inch HD TV is not an emergency because you are having a Super Bowl party and your guests would not be able to comfortably see the game on your 50-inch TV.

If funded properly, IUL can be a very good vehicle to place your emergency fund. Like the bank, the insurance company guarantees that you will not lose money due to investment risk in your cash account. But unlike the bank, IUL also provides you the opportunity to make a higher rate of return based on a market-indexed linked interest so that you can grow your money and keep up with inflation.

From a liquidity standpoint, an IUL is not as liquid as a bank savings account, but most companies can process a withdrawal or loan within a week. This time period should be sufficient for most life emergencies and is enough to avoid our impulsive Super Bowl emergencies.

Before you place your emergency funds into an IUL, it is extremely important to understand the life insurance company's liquidation policies and make sure that you have a sufficient cash surrender value to meet your needs. If this doesn't make sense to you at this point, it should by the end of the book once we cover other material such as maximizing the funding of your policy.

Because of IUL's ability to meet the needs of an emergency fund and provide superior benefits to a bank savings account, the Life Emergency risk gets a checkmark in the Environmental Risk Quadrant.

Legal Issue

There is just no good way of saying it: legal issues suck! Sorry for the French, but many of you understand this intimately. Most people don't realize that legal costs (judgments, settlements, fees) can pile up as much as medical bills can – and generally without insurance protection.

Although tempting, I'm not going to pick on lawyers here (truly, some of my best friends are attorneys), but I will express that I can't think of a less synergistic structure than that of the legal industry. In particular, there is a conflict of interest when it comes to fees. While it is in your best financial interest to minimize the time your attorney spends on your legal issue, it is the goal of attorneys to obtain as many billing hours as they can to maximize revenue. Additionally, the attorney gets to track his or her time without your direct supervision.

Per lawyers.com, the average lawyer charges between $100 and $400 per hour based on experience and geographical area. Based on our previous discussion about emergency funds, it doesn't take a math whiz to figure out legal costs can be crippling Dream Killers.

You may be thinking to yourself that you don't live in circles where you are likely to be involved in a legal matter, but studies show that more than 16 million civil law suits are filed each year in state courts alone, which makes sense considering the U.S. has the highest per capita attorney ratio (300:1) than any other country in the world. (Economic Journal)

I am not an attorney, and this book emphatically does not provide legal advice. I will tell you as a financial planner, however, that the Legal Issue risk is a real one and one that you need to think about.

There are some legal subscription plans that I have found to be of value, which you may consider, but the best guidance I can give you is to protect yourself BEFORE you have legal issues by making sure you have legal documents reviewed before you sign them and/or making sure you have the proper legal advice when you enter a new venture or make a substantial commitment. IUL has many benefits, but make no mistake, it cannot protect you against legal issues.

You may have noticed in our Environmental Risk Quadrant illustration, however, that there is a half checkmark (dash) next to Legal Issue suggesting that IUL partially protects against the risk of legal issues. Let me explain. The reasoning is two-fold. First, due to the liquid aspect of the cash value, IUL is a good instrument to accumulate and access funds in support of legal issues. A larger emergency fund pool, if you will. The second reason is a more meaningful one when we include the idea of creditor protection under the Legal Issue risk.

An often overlooked feature of Indexed Universal Life is creditor protection. While this protection is on a state-by-state basis, generally creditors are limited in their ability to recover judgements from your life insurance cash value. This benefit becomes especially attractive for those who may have high-risk occupations such as doctors or contractors. Again, this book does not provide legal advice, and you need to consult your legal advisor; but because of this feature, IUL receives partial credit in managing the Legal Issue risk.

I will tell you that the IUL policy typically loses its creditor protection if established after a judgement, so you put yourself in a better position when you obtain your policy earlier in the course of implementing your financial plan.

Poor Economy

For those of us who have lived through a recession, we understand what a challenging time it can be.   It becomes a time of great uncertainty in that companies restructure and lay off employees, the stock market can tank causing your accounts to lose value, housing values drop, prices become volatile, and a general feeling of pessimism becomes prevalent leading to great stress for all. As much as the government tries to manage such periods with fiscal and monetary policies, the reality is that recessions cannot be prevented. For whatever reason, the economy naturally plummets every 10-15 years. It's not a matter of "if," it's a matter of when the next recession will occur.

The Financial Pocketknife® helps with a Poor Economy in two ways, financially and emotionally. Financially, an IUL policy offers you many tools to navigate your way through a recession by having the ability to have low-cost access to extra funds if needed, downside market protection, flexible premium payments and low-cost loans. From an emotional perspective, it is equally as powerful in that it provides you with the confidence to know that you are not dependent on an employer for life insurance benefits and have some "cushion" if needed for the possible effects of a Poor Economy.

While there is no foolproof protection against a Poor Economy, IUL does provide flexible options to mitigate the effects, and therefore, gets a partial checkmark.

Job Loss

The loss of a job can be one of the most stressful events in one's life. Unfortunately, in today's global economy and focus on technology, you have a good chance of experiencing it at some point. The Financial Pocketknife cannot protect against Job Loss, but it can help with some of the side effects. Nonetheless, I thought it may be beneficial to share some ideas that might help if you ever find yourself in such a situation.

One important thing to think about if you are employed by a publicly traded company is to make sure you don't own too much company stock. It's very common for employers to promote the company's stock to its employees. Oftentimes, there is unspoken political pressure to own it as well. The message may be given that "If you believe in the company, then surely you would invest in it." This idea is not completely altruistic of many companies but rather a way to increase price support for the stock, in which executives often receive compensation.

The challenge for the employee, however, is when the company experiences a downturn and the employee gets laid off because of "right-sizing." Many times, the company's stock plummets, too, and the employee gets a double whammy by losing her income and having her 401(k) tank.

The most dramatic example of this that I have seen was in the case of Enron. A national TV show highlighted a couple who both worked for Enron. When the company filed for bankruptcy due to fraud, both lost their jobs, and to add insult to injury, both of their retirement plans were wiped out because they were 100% invested in the company's stock. Lesson learned: don't place your retirement plan and family dreams in the hands of your employer.

I suggest not only diversifying your retirement plan but diversifying your income source, too. Whether your spouse seeks employment with a different company or you have a side business, it is a good idea to diversify.

One last point that catches a lot people off guard: when you leave an employer, voluntarily or involuntarily, your benefits end with that company. While this is obvious to most, what people don't understand is that a big problem can occur with group life insurance (your work coverage) and your 401(k).

Group life insurance policies generally allow you to convert your work policy to a personal policy upon termination of your employment. Here's the catch though: you can typically only convert to a permanent policy of their offering and choice (not an IUL) which is going to require additional funds and may not meet your needs based on your goals and strategy. Further, if you decide to purchase a private policy instead, you may not be insurable due to health reasons or may face relatively high rates.

Your 401(k) can have an even bigger poison pill if you have an outstanding loan. Some plans require you to pay back any outstanding loan balance upon termination or have it considered a fully taxable distribution along with penalties if you are under 59 ½ years of age. So, if you borrowed $20,000 from your 401(K) for a down payment on your house and your employment is terminated, you either have to find $20,000 in cash to pay back the loan or accept the $20,000 as a distribution and pay taxes and penalties.

If you have an IUL that your purchased privately, you don't have to worry about having life insurance upon departure and don't have to worry about paying back a policy loan, much less penalty and taxes. We will discuss the 401(k) traps more in Chapter 11.

While the Financial Pocketknife cannot protect you from Job Loss, it can make the event more manageable and alleviate some of the post-employment challenges.

QIII Conclusion

While environmental risk cannot be controlled, the Financial Pocketknife® can help mitigate the effects of a Life Emergency if funded properly. In some circumstances, it may provide assistance with a Legal Issue and a Poor Economy but certainly does not protect against Job Loss. From an emotional perspective, a good argument can be made that it helps provide a sense of security and comfort for each risk.

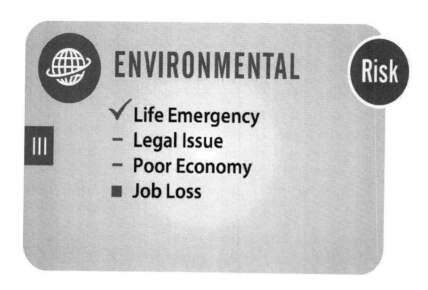

Chapter 8

QIV, It's Personal
(Personal Risks)

If you could kick the person in the pants responsible for most of your trouble, you wouldn't sit for a month.

Theodore Roosevelt

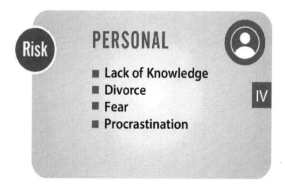

Quadrant IV – Personal Risks

Lack of Knowledge

I'm sure you have noticed by now that I am a big advocate of education. I believe that learning is a lifelong process and that we should continuously seek knowledge. Further, we should constantly sharpen our critical-thinking skills to sift through information and make our own conclusions. Elon Musk refers to critical thinking as "the ability to not be fooled."

Unfortunately, the vast majority of Americans simply lack financial literacy as I have pointed out with statistics throughout the book. Our society doesn't teach personal finance in school and traditional financial professionals ignore most of the population. Here is the good news though.

In today's world of technology, there is little excuse for a Lack of Knowledge. We now have access to more information on our cell phones than the greatest libraries in the world. We can access information anytime, anywhere, in multiple formats within seconds. However, not all information is accurate as we know, so critical-thinking skills become more important than ever before.

There is no way you will ever read one book and become an expert in finance. Nor has it been my intention to make you one by writing this book. I do believe, however, that this book can give you a strong foundational understanding of personal finance. And, if you think about it, the Financial Pocketknife® as a product helps even more with that knowledge base as its features help you understand important financial concepts and declutters the plethora of information that you would have to accumulate if you pursued each feature independently (e.g., index investing, stop losses, life insurance, critical illness, creditor protection, tax minimization, etc.).

For these reasons, I believe that the combination of information you accumulate from the book and financial tools provided by the product earn a full checkmark against the Lack of Knowledge Dream Killer.

Divorce

I already know what you are thinking. You are wondering why I would even talk about the issue of divorce in a financial-themed book and how a financial product can help. The reason I include this issue is because it is a reality that many people face and, as we learned in Chapter 2, it can be financially devastating. According to Forbes, the average cost of divorce is between $15,000 and $30,000. It can truly be a Dream Killer in many significant ways.

As for how IUL combats Divorce, it can't! At least not directly. However, I wouldn't consider it a stretch to suggest that the habits developed and the actions taken in establishing an IUL can certainly help a marriage. Let me explain.

First of all, I believe that purchasing life insurance is a significant act of love. It is a demonstration that one is willing to sacrifice resources that could be used for one's own fulfillment for the benefit of someone other than yourself. When you purchase life insurance, you are making the statement that "I love you so much that I want to make sure that I can care for you even if I can't be with you." Have you ever heard a more romantic line? Okay, maybe not something you would see in a movie, but you get the point.

In contrast, by not having life insurance, aren't you really making an unspoken statement that you really don't care what happens to others if you die? After all, it wouldn't affect you because you would be gone. Isn't if funny, by the way, that divorce decrees typically state that an ex-spouse must obtain and maintain life insurance, but that it is not required while you are married?

While it may still seem like a stretch for you, consider a Citibank survey that found 57% of divorced couples cited money problems as the primary reason for the demise of their marriage. By defining joint dreams and financial goals, establishing a financial foundation and developing the habit of saving and managing your finances, I submit that the Financial Pocketknife® can significantly help a marriage – not directly, but indirectly for sure. Because of this, Divorce gets a half checkmark on our chart.

Fear

In the Dreamworks Animation movie, "The Croods," a prehistoric family spends years sheltered in a dark barren cave constantly in fear of the world outside their immediate surroundings, only to find a vast, lush and fruitful valley nearby in the end. Fear in life is crippling. It may very well be the most powerful Dream Killer of all. It robs you of time and sucks the life out of you. It prevents you from asking out the pretty girl in high school, flying to your dream vacation in Australia, sharing your talents in front of a large audience or starting your business. By living in fear, we fail to live the life God designed us to have.

In fact, social scientists have identified that humans are only born with two fears, the fear of falling and the fear of loud noises. This means that all the other fears we waste our time worrying about are taught to us at some point. Of course, some of these lessons are extremely beneficial and lifesaving (like not jumping on a wild alligator) but other lessons we learn are because of old wives' tales or inaccurate information.

For example, we believe that a job will give us security when, in fact, the average tenure at a job today is 4.7 years. That's a conversation for another book (hint), but the point is, if fear is learned it can also be "unlearned" as well. The key in overcoming fear is to educate yourself and understand the facts of an issue or situation. In my experience, the fear of not knowing something about a potential threat is much worse than the reality of the problem.

I'm certainly not going to make a case that IUL can fix any fear that you have. That would be foolish and absent of any credible reasoning. I do suggest that having a financial strategy in place and having the peace of mind that comes with life insurance, does help you overcome some fears. You no longer need to fear what will happen to your family if you or your spouse dies. You don't need to fear that you will lose your life savings in a stock market crash. You don't have to fear that you can't access money in case of a life emergency. You don't have to fear that creditors can take your life insurance savings away (based on state). You don't have to fear that taxes and inflation will eat away at your retirement. And, you don't have to fear that if you lose your job that you will lose your life insurance as well.

As for parachuting out of a plane or asking out the pretty girl, IUL won't help you with those fears ("The Croods" movie may) but due to the peace of mind acquired from an IUL, we will give the Dream Killer of Fear a half checkmark.

Never let the fear of striking out keep you from coming up to bat.

Babe Ruth

Procrastination

We all struggle with procrastination at times. I have found this particularly true regarding the subject of financial issues. The Financial Pocketknife® cannot help you with Procrastination. Only you can. Perhaps, however, I can help motivate you a bit by showing you the price of Procrastination. Yes, Procrastination has a price. Generally, a big one. This big price is why it is considered a Dream Killer.

If you were to invest $2,400 this year ($200 per month) and were able to get 8% interest each year, in 30 years you would have $24,150. If you wait just one year, that same $2,400 will be worth $22,361 instead (29 years later). This means that it cost you $1,788 because you procrastinated, almost $5 per day.

Perhaps more importantly, you shouldn't assume you have time down the road. This is difficult to relate to when you are younger but when (and if) you reach your middle-aged years, this becomes more apparent as you begin to lose old friends and family members. In fact, that very thing happened with the production of this book. The original editor of this book, a great childhood friend of mine, passed away at age 47.

If you take one thing away from this book, my hope is that you get motived to not let your fears control you, not to procrastinate and chase your dreams regardless of the financial tools you use.

QIV Conclusion

Ultimately, Personal Risks are ones that can only be managed by you. There is no magic product or formula for success. While it may be a little stretch in some cases, the Financial Pocketknife can be a tool to help a Lack of Knowledge, Divorce and Fear, but it simply can't help to fight any of the Dream Killers if you Procrastinate to act on your own behalf.

Risk

PERSONAL

✓ Lack of Knowledge
- Divorce
- Fear
■ Procrastination

Chapter 9
Checklist Checkmate!

Synergy is what happens when one plus one equals ten or a hundred or even a thousand!

Stephen Covey

For those of you who used CliffsNotes back in the day (SparkNotes for millennials), this is the chapter for you. At this point in the book, you should have a firm understanding of the following:

- The severe financial challenges our society faces due to the modern economy, poor government management and the lack of basic financial education
- That individuals have been forced to become more financially astute and responsible for their own financial security due to the loss of traditional pensions, job volatility and instability of Social Security and taxes
- Traditional financial advisors help educate the affluent on financial concepts but ignore the middle class
- Life insurance is not just insurance on your life. It has evolved over time to add all kinds of benefits including assistance with critical, chronic and terminal illnesses, creditor protection, avoidance of probate, tax advantages, inflation hedging, stock market loss protection, favorable loans, liquidity, and cashflow flexibility to name a few.
- Indexed Universal Life insurance synergistically combines multiple financial tools into one super tool to serve as a financial foundation for individuals and families.

Now that we have identified in detail how the Financial Pocketknife® applies to all the Dream Killers individually, let's do a high-level review to see the power of Indexed Universal Life Insurance.

If you recall from the Pregame (Preface), I made a couple of comments about the Financial Pocketknife:

- The goal of this book is to make the "complex" simple!

- The Financial Pocketknife is not suitable for everyone.... But let me state unequivocally, 100%, without a doubt, in my opinion, it is one of the most powerful financial tools ever designed to help families build a strong financial foundation.

In terms of simplification, I hope I have done a good job of defining each risk individually and demonstrating how the risk is managed (or not) by The Financial Pocketknife. The truth is, however, that it will take more than a simple read-through to remember all the details. I've never met a person yet (myself included) who has been able to retain all the details of IUL with just one introduction. Even those with a high financial aptitude will have a challenge remembering all the intricacies for more than a couple of months. The Dream Killer Risk Quadrant™ will be a good visual reminder for you to remember the concepts. And, of course, you can quickly reference each individual risk in the book to activate your memory recall.

PHYSICAL
- ✓ Death
- ✓ Critical Illness
- ✓ Chronic Illness
- ■ Disability
- – Live Too Long

I

FINANCIAL
- ✓ Inflation
- ✓ Market
- ✓ Taxes
- ✓ Liquidity
- – Debt
- – Cash Flow

II

Risk

ENVIRONMENTAL
- ✓ Life Emergency
- – Legal Issue
- – Poor Economy
- ■ Job Loss

III

PERSONAL
- ✓ Lack of Knowledge
- – Divorce
- – Fear
- ■ Procrastination

IV

In reviewing the DKRQ, we see there are many checkmarks and partial checks. Altogether, we identified 19 Dream Killers and categorized them into four types of risk: Physical, Financial, Environmental and Personal. Of these 19 Dream Killers, the Financial Pocketknife® eliminated or significantly mitigated nine risks and had a positive impact in alleviating seven risks. In total, the proper use of Indexed Universal Life Insurance can assist you in achieving your life dreams by positively contributing to 16 of 19 risks (84%).

Understanding all the benefits that Indexed Universal Life Insurance provides to beat the Dream Killers, the question one should ask himself or herself is not "Why should I use it?" but "Why SHOULDN'T I use it?"

Let's think of the alternative of not using IUL for your financial foundation. The first option, which I unfortunately see too often, is to do nothing. As we have discussed, only you can beat the Procrastination Dream Killer. To not be intentional in taking control of your future, is simply not an option if you are serious about achieving your dreams. When people ask me to compare one financial strategy versus another, I certainly have my opinions, but I ultimately share that it is much more important that people take action than it is about the strategy they implement. We will discuss this idea in more detail ahead.

The other option is to use multiple tools to manage all the Dream Killers. With this option, you lose the synergistic qualities of Indexed Universal Life insurance. Sticking with our pocketknife metaphor, you would need to obtain each tool that The Financial Pocketknife® offers individually. This may include (but is not limited to) purchasing term life insurance, obtaining critical and chronic illness supplements, investing in mutual funds, implementing stop-loss techniques, obtaining a line of credit from a bank, using IRAs, annuities, savings accounts, and creating legal documents for various concerns (e.g., probate, creditor protection, estate planning). Think about unbundling all the tools of a pocketknife and putting them in your pocket. Imagine carrying around and keeping up with a screw driver, scissors, knife, tweezers, cork screw, can opener, etc. It certainly wouldn't be convenient, would it? And in some cases, you just can replicate the benefits of IUL with other products.

There are some valid arguments against the use of Indexed Universal Life Insurance based on your goals and circumstances. The most common reasons would include a lack of insurability due to poor health and advanced age with no beneficiaries. Whatever the reason is, however, it is important that you understand the facts from the marketing spin. As we will see in the next chapter, there are many people who are motivated to promote other financial concepts. While many of the arguments against IUL are self-motivated, I believe valid criticisms are good in many ways. If it weren't for criticism and competing ideas, financial strategies and products would never evolve. They would never get better and offer the tremendous benefits they provide today.

Now that we understand the power of IUL, we will review what some of the critics say about it, see how the product can be applied to business scenarios, and how to implement it to meet our goals. Don't stop reading yet! There is a lot of good information to come.

Reminder Stats:

- From its infancy in 2006 through 2016, IUL has grown from 3% of life insurance sales to 21%! (LIMRA)

- While the affluent comprise only about 10% of the population, they account for almost half of the permanent life insurance premiums. (Federal Reserve)

- As wealth increases, so does life insurance ownership. While 56% of non-affluent households own life insurance, up to 82.8% of affluent households own life insurance, including 73.3% of families with more than $5 million in assets. The same holds true for cash value life insurance. While 16.7% of non-affluent own cash value, up to 40.5% of affluent households own cash value. (Federal Reserve, non-affluent equals less than $250,000 in assets).

Chapter 10

The Naysayers

A mind is like a parachute. It doesn't work if it's not open.

Frank Zappa

I believe that open-mindedness and education are key to most things in life. I never shy away from sharing with people the negative aspects of a product or strategy. In fact, I enjoy being challenged on it because it provides me an opportunity to educate others and learn new things myself. I have enough confidence in IUL that I believe when a non-biased person weighs the pros and cons of the advantages and value, he or she will also come to the same favorable conclusion about the benefits.

While I am obviously an ardent advocate for Indexed Universal Life insurance, there are naysayers who vehemently disagree with me. And while I appreciate a good and honest academic debate, I have yet been able to find a good, non-biased argument supporting their assertions. Yes, some of the charges seem very reasonable at first glance, but when you drill down to the details, there is almost always some mischaracterization of the facts or some type of self-interest involved.

While some criticisms are valid, I can assure you that IUL makes some people very nervous based on a lack of knowledge or vested interests. In fact, some very large companies were built on the premise of using alternative products and would have to change their whole business model if they embraced IUL. They even refer to cash value insurance as "trash value" insurance. The challenge for them is that the arguments they used against cash value policies were developed decades ago and are no longer valid as products have evolved to include additional features and benefits. Comically, IUL wasn't even introduced to the public until a little over a decade ago, but these same vested companies try to apply the same tired arguments against it that they did in the 1970s.

In this chapter, we will analyze some of the most popular criticisms of cash value polices (which are often applied to IUL mistakenly) and some of the reasoning behind these claims.

Lack of Knowledge

By far, a lack of knowledge is the greatest commonality I see with the naysayers. To be fair, IUL IS complicated (hence the purpose of this book). Further, you would be amazed at the lack of knowledge that so-called financial experts have regarding IUL. This would include accountants, attorneys, money managers, insurance agents, and yes, the financial gurus on TV and the radio. This is not to bash these professionals, but simply to state that when they make comments on IUL, the statements are often inaccurate.

For example, the use of the term Cash Value to discuss IUL alone is a key indicator that an individual does not have a grasp on the subject. After all, Cash Value (a.k.a. Permanent insurance) could be referring to Whole Life, Variable Life, Variable Universal Life, Universal Life or Indexed Universal Life – all with different features and benefits.

Closed-Mindedness

Financial practices can be like a lot of things in life where closed-mindedness can set in, and we fail to think objectively. Just like politics or sport teams, people tend to be closed-minded and make the critical mistake of reversing the scientific method of proving theories. That is, instead of using data to objectively make a conclusion, humans have a tendency to cherry-pick information and twist data to reach the conclusion that we have been conditioned to believe, want to believe or have a vested interest in.

I was guilty of this early in my career as I would just regurgitate whatever a boss had taught in a Friday training session. It wasn't until I got some experience under my belt that I realized my boss was regurgitating what his boss was saying, who was sharing what the marketing department promoted, who was using information from an industry meeting, and so on and so on. The point is, there is a lot of "group think" that goes on in the industry, and it would amaze you how little time highly educated and seasoned professionals actually take to look at concepts outside their area of specialization, or how closed-minded they are about new concepts. By the way, you would also be surprised about how famous financial gurus on TV and radio get things wrong, too.

Exemptions for Press

The financial services industry is, without a doubt, one of the most heavily regulated industries in the world. It is subject to regulation from the SEC, FINRA, state insurance commissioners, the Department of Labor and banking regulators, just to name a few. However, it might surprise you to know that press members are generally exempt from financial regulation when it comes to reporting.

This exemption not only excludes them from any educational and licensing requirements but gives them free reign to make whatever claim they want regardless of its accuracy or substantiation. Sometimes you will see press members cite an industry expert on a particular financial issue, but reporters commonly offer advice to the masses on financial matters that they have only spent a day or two researching online. Interestingly, many people psychologically give great credence to someone just because they are on the radio or TV. The reality, however, is that many times these reporters have no clue what they are talking about. They have had no formal education or industry experience in finance. They just regurgitate what they found on the internet or from another source.

For professionals in the industry, these financial segments become cringeworthy as we recognize misinformation quickly, but since reporters are exempt from financial regulation, they can really say anything they want regardless of the negative impact it may have on you. Even in the case of educated reporters, there is a big challenge in that they provide uniform advice to everyone watching irrespective of a person's individual needs. There is no "one-size- fits-all" solution to financial advice.

I don't say these things to admonish or demean the professionalism of journalists. In fact, as an advocate of financial education, I would like to see more stories on personal finance. I am simply pointing out that you cannot solely rely on something you heard on the radio or saw on TV and need to consider how it applies to your personal situation.

The Gurus

While we spoke about the press exemption, it is important to address the supposed financial gurus on TV and radio who have strong opinions against cash value polices. For the most part, I think most of these personalities do a great service for much of the general public. Although, I wish they were required to disclose any conflicts of interest they may have with companies and ideas they promote. I don't question the sincerity of these professionals (with maybe the exception of a well-known one who has a new book out every week). Professional opinions, unquestionably, differ on subject matter. I will say, however, that they are simply wrong when it comes to their bashing of cash value insurance. They may say it loudly and definitively, but that doesn't make the statement correct. Specifically, you will notice in their analysis a few common mistakes which you may recognize now that you understand some of the concepts we discussed.

First, they do not compare apples to apples. In one example, they will compare the use of mutual funds to a low fixed-rate whole life policy and fail to address tax consequences upon distribution (especially if under 59 ½). As we have learned, IUL does not solely have a fixed interest rate and has significant tax savings.

Second, they make the assumption that by the time a term policy ends, you will have accumulated enough wealth to self-insure your family in the event of your death and have plenty of money for retirement. As statistics cited in this book suggest, this assumption is a very bad one as most people continue to struggle in their later years. The fact is, most people who purchase term insurance do not save and invest the difference. Instead, they find something else to spend the difference on. Often, they find themselves in need of life insurance later in life but can no longer qualify for it for health reasons. Or, they learn that the cost of insurance is too high at a later age, and they can't afford it.

In addition to the assertion that life insurance is no longer needed as you accumulate wealth, they are disregarding all the additional benefits of IUL we identified such as creditor protection and downward market protection, just to name a couple.

Last, and perhaps most importantly, they don't know your individual circumstances and needs. They don't know what you are trying to accomplish. They don't know your current financial situation. They don't know your health status. They don't know who is dependent on you. They don't know your source of income. They don't know your budget, etc., etc. There is no cookie cutter solution for everyone!

Common Criticisms

When the naysayers speak about cash value life insurance, their criticism is based on three contentions: the idea that cash value insurance is expensive, that you can achieve a higher rate of return in a mutual fund, and that you only need life insurance for a limited period of time. Ultimately, these arguments are used to promote the concept of "Buying Term and Investing the Difference."

We need to remember that these arguments were developed based on whole life policies decades ago. But as we have learned, IUL is not a whole life policy. Rather, it is an evolution of whole life insurance that has benefits and features that were never imagined when these arguments were developed. Yet, the naysayers try to link the same criticisms to IUL with little validity.

Cash Value Insurance Is Expensive

To be clear, IUL policies can have a lot of expenses. Often, these expenses can concern consumers to the point where they understandably become a turn-off. While the expenses can seem large at times, they are often misunderstood and/or exaggerated by the marketing spin of competing product marketers. Let's look at some common expenses of IUL and then discuss how and why these expenses get manipulated.

First, it should be understood that expenses associated with IUL policies vary greatly from company to company, and each company may have multiple IUL product versions designed for different objectives. For instance, a company may

117

have one IUL designed to focus on cash accumulation and another version that is designed with a larger emphasis on benefits.

The expenses can definitely make a difference in your policy's performance over the long-run so it is important to review the expenses listed in your policy illustration. Here are a few commons expenses charged for IUL polices:

- Premium Expense Charge (Load) – This is a charge that is applied as a percentage of premium based on contributions. Similar to a mutual fund, the charge can be in the range of 5% on premiums. Unlike mutual funds, the charge may be reduced or eliminated altogether after a number of years. This is where IUL offers an extreme advantage in the later years. It is common for companies to combine other expenses (that we mention below) into the load, which can make the expense look very high. But remember, they are just using a different categorization for the expense and not necessarily out of line with the total expenses charged in the policy.

It should also be noted that some policies may have no premium loads at all. Often, these policies are part of a comprehensive portfolio where a fee is charged on the amount of assets under management instead of commission.

- Monthly Administration Fees – $8 range for statements, service, etc.

- Monthly Expense Charge – Based on a percentage of assets. These are very low, in the neighborhood of 0.05% per month.

- Cost of Insurance Charge – Your insurance charge based on each $1,000 of your death benefit coverage. This is a standard type of charge no matter what kind of life insurance you purchase.

- Surrender Charges – Surrender charges occur if you cancel (surrender) your policy before the surrender period, which can last a long time, typically up to 15 years. These charges can be brutal in the early years but decrease in percentage terms each year. It should be noted and understood that these charges do not mean that you cannot take money out of the policy in the early years (without paying the surrender charge) but that you have to keep the policy active (in force). The good news about this charge is that you get to decide if you pay for it.

While I used to really dislike these charges, I have changed my mindset over the years. Not because I don't think the charges are exorbitant, but because I believe it forces people to develop strong savings habits and ultimately acts in their own best interest in the long-run.

Remember, IUL is a long-term strategy with great flexibility in premium payment. If you are not comfortable committing to the premium amount, you should probably make some adjustments to the face amount (death benefit) before you acquire the policy. If you do find yourself in a position where you think you need to cancel your policy early, you should contact your agent and/or insurance company to see if there are any options for you to keep the policy. In some cases, the insurance company may reduce your face amount which would decrease the premium amounts and avoid the surrender charges.

If you are older with adult beneficiaries (e.g., adult children), you may want to consider giving them the option of paying the premiums, instead of surrendering the policy, to protect their inheritance. This may seem a little awkward to discuss but can be a win-win for all and is not an uncommon practice.

While IUL policies certainly have their share of expenses, the critics often fail to make an accurate comparison as they will compare apples to oranges. Since the objective of this book is to keep things simple, I won't go into all the technical arguments on expenses but let me suggest that looking at expenses alone is the wrong way to analyze financial (or life) decisions. The true factor that should be focused on when making a decision is the VALUE it produces, not the expense. Let me explain.

You see, to determine "Value," one must also consider the "output" (return) that came from the "input" (expense). So, while expenses are important and should be understood, one cannot say that something is expensive without considering the output that creates its value. Think of it this way. If I were to tell you that a Harley

Davidson was expensive because I can buy a Huffy bicycle at Walmart for $100, you would probably laugh at me because I would be ignoring the output (automation, comfort, style, brand, speed, quality) that a Harley provides to create value. Likewise, I can't say IUL is expensive without considering the value it brings (e.g., Living Benefits, Loan Options, Market Protection, Tax Savings, Liquidity). By the way, value doesn't just have to be in monetary terms. It can also include non-monetary factors such as one's personal health or emotional peace of mind.

As a young professional at a prominent mutual fund company, I received a complaint call from a shareholder regarding the fees charged in a particular "developing markets" fund. This fund was more expensive than average (1.90% vs. 1.55%) mostly due to the added cost of making international trades, but here's the thing, the fund was up 94% for the year. Yes, 94%! While I appreciated the client's focus on expense, my real thought was, "Are you kidding me?! Let me get this right; you have literally almost doubled your money in one year, and you are complaining about an additional 0.35% charge for trading?" I really thought he was joking with me at first. I explained to him the reason for the higher expense (international trading fees), but he still argued. Finally, I offered him a simple solution. I explained that I could retroactively reallocate his investment to another fund with a lower charge but also with a lower return of only 18%. I was bluffing, of course, as this really wasn't an option, but to no surprise the light bulb went on for the client and he realized that the value of netting over 94% in one year was certainly worth the extra 0.35% charge.

Yes, cash value insurance can have substantial charges, but it can also provide incredible value. For instance, let's say someone made an "expensive" premium payment of $200 in their first month of coverage and died, leaving their family a death benefit of $500,000. That financial return would be almost 250,000%. Would one still say the policy was expensive?

Okay, so that example may be an extreme case and could also be applied to term insurance. But again, the focus should be on value, not expense. We could easily make similar arguments for the tax savings benefits, loan features, creditor protection and market protection. In fact, market protection is one of my favorite comparisons as it is a unique feature of IUL, and in my view, can be worth all the expenses by itself.

Let's say you picked your own no-load mutual fund, which had very low management fees of 1%. Due to a bear market, those funds lost 30% in one year. Couldn't we conclude that your actual cost of having that fund was really 31%? And, wouldn't it make sense that any cost for an alternative investment lower than 31% would actually provide you with more value? Again, the focus needs to be on value, not expense.

Mutual Funds Provide a Superior Investment Return

The original criticism that mutual funds could offer a superior investment return compared to whole life products over the long run WAS completely true when the argument was first used decades ago. And, it should be true because whole life insurance, as we have learned, is a policy type that has no stock market exposure but rather provides a fixed interest rate, just like a bank CD. This assertion is the ultimate example of deception because it does not make a valid comparison of like investments.

You, however, are equipped to not fall for this trick because you now know from previous chapters that IUL is not a fixed-rate policy but offers returns tied to the stock market. (See Chapter 6, *Offense AND Defense*, for a refresher course.) Perhaps more importantly, IUL protects against negative stock market returns unlike equity-based mutual funds.

When comparing mutual funds to IUL, you must also consider the mutual funds charges and fees and taxation of earnings. As you can see, the superior return argument for mutual funds is no longer valid in today's world.

Life Insurance is Only Needed for a Period of Time

A popular argument against cash value (permanent) insurance is that you only need insurance for a specific period of time, typically to cover a large liability. For example, you use a 30-year term policy to cover the financial obligation of a 30-

year mortgage. A secondary argument to this idea is that you will accumulate enough wealth when term insurance expires to be able to self-insure against the death of a breadwinner.

To suggest that life insurance is only needed for a temporary period of time is to assume you will become independently wealthy by the end of the term period and is a failure to recognize all the benefits of IUL, including living benefits, investment options, loan provisions, probate avoidance, etc. We will address this issue in more detail when we discuss "Term vs. Perm," but as you can see, the assertion is false.

Buy Term and Invest the Difference

The strategy of "buying term and investing the difference" has been used for years and has been a big point of contention among professionals and TV personalities. While this method was developed in the late 1970s and made a lot of sense at the time, financial products have evolved over the past 40 years, and the answer isn't so clear anymore. Term insurance can certainly be a valuable tool (and sometimes is used to enhance The Financial Pocketkknife strategy), but it also exposes you to great uncertainty in the future, especially if you are unable to accumulate enough assets for retirement and/or cannot qualify for coverage in your later years. Further, there are many other features that are offered in IUL that may not be available in other products such as tax free distributions, favorable loans and guarantees to prevent market loss.

The proponents of buying term and investing the difference, most always lead with the argument that cash value (permanent) insurance is too expensive. They then play to one's emotions by insinuating that the life insurance company is ripping you off with cash value life insurance with a further implication that wise people use term and invest the difference for superior results (meaning you are foolish if you don't buy term and invest the difference). These arguments are completely misleading and flat out incorrect.

The idea of cash value (of which IUL is a subset) being expensive is, in part, a misnomer. While proponents are quick to point out the large difference of premium between term and cash value, they do not point out that the cash value premium includes a savings component. They simply are not comparing apples to apples, and therefore, are being misleading in their claim. Further, they conveniently fail to mention the expenses associated with investing the difference or consider the total long-term costs. For instance, since cash value products cover you for your entire life, many cash value products will offset the higher insurance costs of the later years with a larger relative premium in the early years. Based on this practice, cash value insurance can actually be less expensive than term insurance based on comparing apples to apples for the entirety of an insureds life. Last, as we discussed in detail, expenses are important but the value of a financial tool is really the most important element to consider.

It's easy bait for an agent to make the emotional charge that "Insurance companies are ripping you off" with cash value policies. No one likes to be taken advantage of or get ripped off, especially by entities that are often demonized by our society (rather undeservedly in my view but not our focus here). Very simple logic, however, can quickly dispel this myth. Most life insurance companies offer both types of life insurance products, term and cash value. These products are actuarily designed to produce the same rate of return for companies. Common sense dictates that a company would not invest resources into a lesser product (regardless of the industry) if they can obtain substantially higher returns from another product. Therefore, if you make the argument that life insurance companies are ripping people off on cash value polices, we also have to hold true that the same logic applies to the term policies. Ironically, the few insurance companies that promote this claim are known to have the most expensive term products in the industry.

The insinuation that "wise people buy term insurance" is also false. Let's review the following statistics on life insurance ownership based on policy type.

- 2017 U.S. Individual Life Insurance – Product Market Share by Premium

  Term –　　21%

  Cash Value – 79% (IUL, UL, VUL, WL)

  Source: LIMRA's U.S. Retail Individual Life Insurance Sales Summary Report, Fourth Quarter 2017

- As wealth increases, so does its ownership. While 16.7% of non-affluent own it, up to 40.5% of affluent households own it. (Federal Reserve)

By logic, to accept the idea that "term insurance is used by wise people," you would have to agree that the overwhelming majority of Americans are stupid, and intelligence actually decreases as wealth increases. For those of you who have experienced driving in my home base of Tampa Bay, you might agree with this assertion, but the reality is that it would be "unwise" to accept such a thought process.

To be extremely clear, I am not stating that term insurance is not a good tool or that one is unintelligent if they use term insurance. There are proper uses for term insurance, and I own term polices myself (in addition to cash value). However, for one to make a blanket statement about term being superior to cash value is simply false and/or misleading.

With the myriad of factors and opinions to consider, you may be asking, "Which type of life insurance should I use?"

The good news is that I can give you a guaranteed definitive answer on which method is best for you. I just need you to answer four questions with 100% accuracy.

1. When are you going to die?
2. Who will be financially dependent on you when that day occurs?
3. How much liquid money will you have at that time?
4. How much money will your dependents need to maintain their same living standard indefinitely?

If you can 100%, without a doubt, answer these four questions, then you will not be eligible to purchase life insurance in the first place because it would mean that you have some sort of terminal illness or represent an uninsurable risk profile.

Assuming that you don't know the answer to these questions, it becomes pretty obvious that permanent insurance should be a consideration for most everyone. However, the best way to see which strategy makes sense for your personal objectives is to have an illustration created that compares the two strategies in numerical terms. I can't emphasize enough though, that when comparing strategies, you must be careful to compare apples to apples.

Apples to Apples

Mark Twain popularized the line, "There are three kinds of lies: lies, damned lies and statistics." Shocker alert: data can be manipulated to support an argument. Unfortunately, this happens all the time in financial presentations. Sometimes this is done unintentionally, but many times it is done to make one's product and/or strategy seemingly more attractive. While there are too many industry methods to manipulate data outside the scope of this book, one thing to make sure you review is interest and tax rates. For example, one product may be comparing its strategy with one rate of return (on the investment) with a lower rate on another product. Likewise, you may see comparisons that don't show the effect of taxes on your distributions.

While data can be manipulated and a lot of variables have to be considered, in the end, it's relatively easy to evaluate a strategy. Just look at the numbers. A good agent should be able to show you detailed financial comparisons of different strategies. Just make sure they compare apples to apples based on the points you learned in the book.

Sales Psychology

With the technical arguments covered, I would like to share with you the most common sales techniques used by "Term Promoters" to sell term insurance. When I talk about term promoters, I am referring to those agents who only sell term insurance and bash the concept of cash value insurance. Typically, these agents are associated with companies who don't even offer cash value products. The fact is that the recommendation of term insurance is an easy story to sell, leading to more sales and commission for agents.

Frankly, helping a client with products that they NEED can be quite challenging. It's not easy to convince and motivate people to do things that they SHOULD do rather than things they WANT to do. If it were, there would be no such thing as cigarettes, lotteries or Twinkies, and McDonald's would sell kelp smoothies. Taking the time to teach a client about the benefits of IUL, convincing them to sacrifice other wants to develop a long-term savings plan, and prompting them to start the application process can be exhausting. It is much, much easier to just do the easy thing and sell them term.

Think about it. Would you rather spend valuable time learning the details about something you find boring and commit more money to an IUL product, or would you rather hear an agent tell you, "Don't let that evil insurance company rip you off! All you need is a cheap term policy that will only require 10 minutes of your time to submit an application"?

Heck, I would jump on that proposition myself if I didn't know any better.

Another popular line used by term promoters is: "The only reason another agent would show you a cash value policy is because they make a huge commission on you!" While it is true the agent typically makes more commission on a cash value policy due to several factors (which really shouldn't be an argument to consider if you receive a benefit as well), the implication is that the agent is a crook who is selling you a product with no value, just for his or her own financial gain.

You can see how playing on a client's emotions by using scare tactics and providing an "easy and cheap" solution is much easier than getting the client to do what they NEED to do. The problem is that this negative approach is not only unprofessional and lazy but may not be in your best interest based on your individual goals and objectives.

From the term promoter's perspective, however, it is all a numbers game. He may make less money per sale but will make up for it in volume by making the "easy sell" and moving on to the next guy.

The true professional will review your financial needs, take the time to educate you on all the options (IUL and Term) and make a recommendation based on the best fit for you. We will cover this more in Chapter 12, *Putting It all Together.*

THE Best Financial Product for Everyone ... NOT!

Now that we understand the many great features of The Financial Pocketknife®, you may be asking yourself, "Why wouldn't everyone want to own this product?" The answer is that not everyone can qualify for the product, nor is it a suitable product for everyone.

While The Financial Pocketknife can provide a strong financial foundation for families and has many tremendous benefits, it is not a solution for everyone. In fact, when you hear someone tell you that there is a "one-size-fits-all" product or strategy for everyone, you should be very skeptical. Each of us has our own unique financial objectives and preferences. The only way to determine if a financial instrument is suitable for your individual situation is to examine your own financial goals, have a personalized illustration created on your behalf and analyze if the strategy meets your objectives.

Your health status is a key determinant of how well Indexed Universal Life will meet your needs, if at all. While the greater your health, the better the product will perform, the only way to complete the analysis will be to go through the underwriting process once you have applied. But for the most part, a personalized illustration will help you determine how the plan may benefit you and to what degree.

Chapter 11

The 401(k) Trojan Horse

Beware of false knowledge; it is more dangerous than ignorance.
George Bernard Shaw

It is estimated that 54 million Americans are invested in 401(k) accounts with $5.2 trillion in assets (Investment Company Institute, 2017). Yes, that is trillion with a "T." These plans, along with their sibling plans for non-for-profits and government employees (403 (b) and 457), have become the de facto retirement plans for the public. They are often cited in the media as a barometer of how well Americans are doing financially, considered a rite of passage for adulthood and generally accepted as the best way for individuals to save for retirement. In fact, many companies have automatic enrollment into the plans in which one must "opt-out" if he or she chooses not to participate.

These plans are marketed as a way to save on taxes while receiving the "generous" bonus of matching employer contributions. Although there are strong benefits derived from these plans, most people have never really analyzed their effectiveness compared to other financial concepts. Nor are they aware of some very negative attributes of these plans, until they get surprised by them.

To get the full picture on 401(k)s, it's helpful to understand the motivations of employers and the government to promote these plans. If you believe that it is because they are acting in your best interest, I have a bridge to sell you. The truth is that the introduction of these plans is a way for employers to transfer risk and expense to the employees and an opportunity for the government to collect even more taxes. In fact, we could make a strong argument that these plans are really a Trojan Horse in disguise.

Trojan Horse: a trap intended to undermine an enemy (Dictionary.com)

Note: for purposes of the following discussion, we will use the term 401(k) interchangeably with other types of retirement plans, e.g., 403(b).

To understand the 401(k) Trojan Horse, we need to establish a couple of terms and review a brief history of employer retirement plans. For the greater part of the 20th century, companies provided pension plans for their employees, also known as "defined benefit" plans because they would pay a defined amount of income to a worker after he retired. To provide this benefit, employers would contribute to the plan yearly and be responsible for managing the plan so that the employee would receive his pension payments upon retirement. Notice that the employer was responsible for ALL the contributions and ALL the investment risk. The downside for the employee was that he had to stay with the company to receive the benefit, could not take the balance of the plan if he left the company before retirement and could not access it before retirement. The big risk that the employee had was that if the company went out of business, he could lose his pension (although the government put in some safeguards to mitigate).

The 1980s brought the best music in history and the proliferation of 401(k) plans. Unlike defined benefit plans, 401(k)s allowed employees to have portability with their retirement plan, access to money before retirement, mitigate the risk of losing their pension due to company bankruptcy and possibly grow their account even more because of being able to direct their own investments. With the 401(k) option, as you probably know, the employee is required to make their own contribution – hence, the name "defined contribution plan." As you can see, to participate in the 401(k) plan, the employee assumed much of the financial contribution (in some cases all) and the investment risk. The graph below demonstrates how companies over time have phased out pensions and introduced 401(k)s.

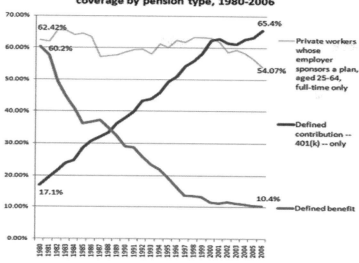

Figure 3: Percentage of private sector workers with pension coverage by pension type, 1980-2006

Source: Center for Retirement Research, 2009.

Now, maybe I am just not idealistic enough to believe that companies replaced pensions with 401(k)s solely for the benefit of their employees and not for themselves. After all, not only do 401(k)s benefit employees financially but they also provide valuable employees the freedom to leave the company for better opportunities and take their pension with them (yes, this is said sarcastically).

I am not a corporate basher by any means and understand that, in reality, companies are in business to make a profit and have to compete. Eliminating pensions simply means more profit for the companies, plain and simple. And once a company's competitors have a profit advantage by eliminating their pension plan, it must consider the same option to remain competitive.

But just because it's better for the company, doesn't mean it's worse for you. Or does it? I am a big believer in life not being a zero-sum game, that it is possible to have win-win scenarios. Statistics, however, show that Americans are struggling greatly in the retirement game. As we have discussed, they just don't save as they should and aren't equipped to manage their own "pension fund." Further, due to misguided fiduciary regulations, most advisors won't provide advice on 401(k)s despite evidence that consumers do much better with help.

Aside from the personal discipline factor, 401(k)s have other little-known deficiencies. For example, what about the tax savings that are so perpetuated? With a traditional 401(k), you don't pay current income tax on contributions, and earnings on your account are accumulated tax-deferred until you make a withdrawal. At that time, you get taxed at your ordinary income tax rate, regardless of whether the proceeds were from your original contribution or investment returns. Here's are the hidden problems with 401(k)s.

Capital gains from investment returns are typically taxed at a lower rate than the rate you pay for income tax. So, in effect, you are really paying a higher tax rate for deferring your capital gains. And while you may have access to your account before you retire, you get to pay an additional 10% penalty on top of your ordinary income tax if you do.

Think about the scenario of getting laid off from your job. The good news is that you can access your funds if needed to help pay for things while you find another job. The bad news is, you get to pay income tax (let's assume 20% for discussion) and a 10% early withdrawal penalty to access your money in your family's time of financial distress. That's right, at the time of your greatest need, you get to pay 30% to the government. Who would ever think that's a good deal? Especially when it can be avoided altogether if you had savings in an IUL where you can legally avoid income taxes and penalties upon withdrawal (via loan). (Refer to Chapter 4, *The Financial Pocketknife®* for a refresher on loans and taxation of IUL.)

You might be thinking, "I can take a loan from my 401(k), too!" That's partially true. Here's the kicker (you'll love this one!). While it is true you can take a loan from your 401(k), in most circumstances, you can only take the loan while you are still employed. That's right. Once you leave an employer, the loan option normally goes bye-bye. So, if you get laid off or terminated, you only have the option of making a taxable withdrawal if you need the money. You cannot avoid the taxes or penalty by taking a loan, even though it is your own money. But wait, it gets even worse!

If you already have an outstanding loan, some plans require you to pay back the loan upon termination. Otherwise, your outstanding loan becomes counted as a distribution and you get a tax bill for it along with a premature distribution penalty if you are younger than 59 ½. So in this scenario, you may have borrowed $30,000 for a down payment on your home and upon termination of your employment, you have to pay back the entire outstanding balance of the loan within a short period of time (say two months depending on the plan) or get taxed on the distribution (up to $9,000 due in taxes based on our scenario assumptions).

One last brief but important comment on the taxation of traditional 401(k)s. Depending on your age, you are generally better to pay taxes on the contribution rather than the distribution because over time, the majority of your account accumulation comes from compound interest. This leads to higher total taxes paid if you pay upon distribution. As we commonly say in the industry, you'd rather get taxed on the seed than the harvest. So, if you do invest in a 401(k), you are typically better to choose a Roth 401(k) if it is available to you. Of course, you are able to mimic the same tax treatment in an IUL by using loans that are provided by a Roth 401(k), so the Roth still doesn't have an advantage over the IUL in that aspect.

So, when does a 401(k) make sense? The answer depends on your employer's matching of contributions.

Take the Match

Occasionally, I will hear advisors (or other books) promote the idea that 401(k)s should not be used at all and that a cash value life insurance policy is always a better alternative. I really dislike these types of statements and marketing ploys. To be clear, that is not the idea I am suggesting at all.

Generally speaking, I advise that people take advantage of a 401(k) if the employer matches the employee's contributions. After all, a 100% match on your money is hard to beat under any scenario. The amount you contribute over the employer match level, however, is very debatable based on your individual goals. For example, if the employer matches 100% of your contribution up to 3% of your salary, you more than likely should contribute up to the 3% level so that you receive the employer match. Then, consider an IUL for any additional contributions above the 3% match.

Most importantly, only consider using an IUL as an alternative to your 401(k) if you have a need for life insurance. Remember, IUL policies are meant first and foremost to be life insurance, not a primary investment vehicle. And one last tip, if a financial representative advises you to make a taxable withdrawal from your 401(k) and place it into a cash value live insurance policy, it's probably time to find a new advisor unless you are already retired and doing so for legacy planning.

Business Funding

Many people have the entrepreneurial dream of starting their own business. Typically, the largest hindrance to this dream is the need for capital. As the saying goes, "You have to have money to make money." For better or for worse, a common way of funding a new business is via one's 401(k). As we know, however, when you liquidate assets from a 401(k), the distribution is taxed as ordinary income and subject to a 10% penalty for early distribution if you are under 59 ½ years old.

Moreover, the IRS does not allow you to invest the 401(k) assets into your start-up company's stock as a source of funding (there is a controversial technique for doing so but not our focus here). Think about that for a second. You can essentially give control of your money to the CEO of a publicly traded company but cannot use your own money to invest in your own business. (And we wonder why small businesses struggle so much in this country.)

Based on these provisions, to use your own hard-earned money saved over years of sacrifice as capital for a new venture, it will either cost you greatly in taxes (making your cost of capital greater than most credit cards) or force you to find another source of funds. And, if you are thinking of a home equity loan, or a business loan for that matter, you will need collateral and a source of income, which is not common during the start-up phase.

Alternatively, if you have built up your cash value in your IUL, you can borrow from yourself (see Chapter 3 as a refresher) without paying taxes, without paying a premature distribution penalty, and without having to qualify.

In addition to the shortcomings of 401(k) plans that we have discussed in this chapter, remember too, that IUL also offers additional benefits that 401(k) cannot, including guaranteed downside protection on market risk, no predefined limits on contributions and superior loan provisions.

The decision to use an IUL instead of a 401(k) is, of course, an important one that has to take into consideration many technical factors and individual objectives. Remember, everyone is unique and this book is not intended to give individual advice, but I think it certainly makes sense to discuss your options with your professional advisors.

Chapter 11.5
The Secret Chapter –
Advanced Markets

I like to say it's an attitude of not just thinking outside the box, but not even seeing the box.

Safra A. Catz

Welcome to the Secret Chapter! I know you are wondering why I would hide this chapter from the table of contents. This chapter is specifically directed to business owners and/or those with more advanced estate planning needs, and therefore, not the focus of most readers. If these criteria don't apply to your current situation, go ahead and skip to the next chapter. If it does apply to you, however, you may want to consider some very useful business applications for IUL. I will not provide a lot of detail on the subject matter but do want to address some concepts that may deserve a more detailed discussion with your financial professionals. Plus, by sneaking this chapter in, I get to test my adult kids to see if they actually read the book when I give it to them.

The term "Advanced Markets" or "Advanced Sales" in the life insurance industry refers to life insurance used in business planning and/or estate planning. For business uses, life insurance is typically used to assist in transferring a business upon the death of a founder, incentivizing and retaining key employees, or as a retirement plan alternative for owners and employees. For estate planning purposes, life insurance is often used to fund trusts for charitable purposes, mitigate tax issues, protect assets or leave legacy gifts.

Business Funding

As we discussed in the last chapter, which compared 401(k)s to IUL, IUL can be a good source of business funding. If you have built up your cash value in your IUL, you can borrow from yourself (see Chapter 4 as a refresher) without paying taxes, without paying a premature distribution penalty and without having to qualify.

Small Business Retirement Plan

Employers use 401(k)s as a way to attract and retain employees. As we discussed in the last chapter, employers like these plans because they are cheaper than traditional pension plans. This, however, does not hold true for small employers. Due to various regulations, administrative expenses can be costly and employers are required to allow all employees to participate (with few exceptions). Many times, small employers do not have the scale to make these plans feasible. Cash value life insurance becomes a great option for small employers to use instead of 401(k)s.

Non-Qualified Deferred Compensation: Your business utilizes cash value life insurance to fund an agreement providing specified benefits payable at a future event, such as retirement, death or disability of a key employee.

Key Person Insurance

Many businesses employ "key" people who have a significant impact on the business being successful. For example, a sales executive who is responsible for a significant share of revenue or COO who keeps the business running smoothly. If a key employee were to be hit with the proverbial bus or leave for another opportunity, the company would face serious financial consequences. Key Person Insurance funded by IUL can establish golden handcuffs for a key employee by creating a long-term bonus fund for the employee and/or paying a death benefit to the business to help offset any financial distress that may be caused if the employee died before retirement.

Buy-Sell Agreement - Succession Planning

Small business owners can cause havoc for their families and business stakeholders when they die. Oftentimes, family members are not qualified to take over the business while capable employees cannot afford to buy the business.

As a result, the business ends up being sold for less than optimal value or is forced to shut down. All of which can be avoided rather easily by having a Buy-Sell Agreement in place and using an IUL policy to facilitate the sale of the business upon an owner's death.

Estate Planning

Advanced Markets also includes the practice of Estate Planning. IUL is a popular tool for Trusts, Estate Tax concerns and Charitable Giving.

All of these issues can become fairly complex and typically require the assistance of legal and tax professionals in addition to your financial advisor. The good news, however, is that every reputable life insurance company has an Advanced Marketing team who will help you at no cost. These teams are typically comprised of estate planning attorneys and financial professionals who specialize in these issues and work on these types of scenarios with clients every day. Your financial advisor should be your "quarterback" in these cases and coordinate for you. It would be wise to take advantage of these services if any of the concepts we discussed fit your personal scenario.

Chapter 12
Putting It All Together

A good plan violently executed now is better than
a perfect plan executed next week.
George S. Patton

Now that we understand what Dream Killers are and how IUL combats them, we need to understand how we put all this information together and implement a plan to maximize our opportunity.

A quick review from previous chapters will remind us that the goal of this book is to help you achieve your individual dreams. Therefore, the first thing I have my clients do has nothing to do with numbers. Instead, I have them define their dreams. As Stephen Covey taught, begin with an end in mind.

1. Complete a Life Assessment: 6 Fs and SMART GOALS

As we discussed in Chapter 1, if we don't know our destination, there is little probability that we will ever get there. It is important that you spend a lot of time really thinking this through what you want in life. It truly is an investment in yourself and your family. I highly recommend you do this exercise with your spouse. Ideally, you want to get away somewhere for the weekend, leave the kids at home and turn off the world. Really do some soul searching and be as specific and as detailed as possible. Remember, you may visit our website and download a copy of our Dream Planner that includes the 6 Fs.

Another method I recommend when developing your goals is to be SMART. SMART is an acronym for:

141

S – Specific (Define as clearly as possible)

M – Measurable (Quantify as much as possible)

A – Attainable (Make sure it is realistic; for example, I may want to pitch for the Tampa Bay Rays, but it's probably not going to happen in my late 40s)

R – Relevant (The goal should be relevant to your life mission; for example, is learning how to juggle while riding a unicycle really worth the time investment for the bigger picture?)

T – Time (Set a target date for completion)

Example of a SMART Goal:

Instead of: I want to pay for my kid's college.

Use: I will save $50,000 dollars by August 1, 2030, for my daughter Katie to obtain her bachelor's degree.

Notice that I am not only very specific with my statement, but I also changed the wording to reflect an affirmative statement of "I will" instead of "I want." This is very powerful as it transforms your mindset and adds accountability. As Yoda said, "Do" or "Do Not." There is no "Try." (Yes, I translated from whatever language he speaks, but you get the idea.)

Not to get off on a tangent, but no, you don't have to define the school or major, and yes, it is okay to put a limit on what you will pay for college. I've seen many people get into a lot of financial trouble making bad "college investments." I can also tell you as a college professor, I have observed that those who have to work a little bit in college (and struggle) tend to be the better students and more successful as adults.

Last, I differ from the norm a bit in that I suggest people define their goals before they do their budget. The main reason for that is so you don't shrink your vision thinking about your dreams. We do need to prioritize, of course, but let's get clarity in what we want to accomplish in life before we analyze and limit our dreams based on budget constraints.

2. Prepare a Personal Budget

I am willing to predict that you just cringed when you saw the word "budget." But don't! It is rare these days to see a client who actually does a budget, much less follows it. But with today's technology, it doesn't have to be a difficult task. There are several technology companies (and financial institutions) that offer account aggregation and budgeting. Specifically, these services will track all your transactions from all your payment accounts (bank accounts, credit cards, etc.), categorize them, and automatically show you your spending habits. Of course, you can just put a pencil to paper as well, but I suggest leveraging the power of technology. While I don't endorse any companies, I would recommend you do a simple internet search and research your options.

You also don't need to have your budget down to the penny. Of course, the more detail the better, but many people give up on creating a budget because they find the level of detail takes more time than they want to spend. You just need a good estimate of what you are spending your money on. The results from the budgeting process may surprise you quite a bit, especially when you see how much you pay for transportation and food.

3. Find a Qualified Advisor/Agent

I am a big believer in the use of professionals regardless of the task. If you ever did a home project, there is a good chance you agree with me. While it may be alright to make a mistake tiling a floor, putting tent film on your windows or creating your own website, some things are just too important to "Do It Yourself." I'm not going to operate on myself if I need knee surgery, I'm not going to represent myself in a legal matter, I'm not going to change the brakes on my Lamborghini (or Toyota), and I'm not going to manage my own financial matters. It is simply too important, and in my opinion, not wise.

Not only do studies demonstrate that those who use financial professionals are more successful over time, but my decades of experience suggest the same. I can't tell you how many times I have seen people think they can develop their own trading system, read something off the internet, follow the opinion of a family member, or listen to a radio show and believe they are more knowledgeable than professionals who have formally studied financial subjects and have worked in the industry day in and day out for decades. Unfortunately, and inevitably, something blows up, and it's not pretty when it does. (Like when my wife tried to cut my hair instead of my stylist to save a couple of bucks when we first got married.)

Another reason to use a professional is to provide a different perspective and minimize emotion. It's always easier to objectively analyze a situation when you don't have a dog in the fight. I remember a former boss of mine in the industry who was the CEO of a multibillion dollar life insurance company. He told me how his financial planner suggested he do something, and I was completely confused. I asked him why he would pay a financial planner to manage his financial affairs considering he was the CEO of a financial company and had 40 years of experience. He explained to me that his planner freed up his time so he could focus on running the company, provided a different perspective, and took the emotions out of the subject matter. That struck me as very wise. And, that's the difference between smart and wise. Smart people may be able to do things on their own, but wise people hire professionals.

I believe a key reason people avoid professionals is that they just don't know how to find a good one. By good one, I mean one who is competent and trustworthy. There are a few things you should look for in a competent IUL agent. First, you are not likely to find them in traditional banks or brokerage firms. If you bank at a large institution that has a financial advisor, chances are they are not familiar with IUL, much less experts. The same holds true for financial advisors who are primarily asset managers or stock brokers. You need to understand that just like the medical or legal fields, the financial services industry is highly specialized. You wouldn't go see a dentist for a heart problem, and similarly, you wouldn't see a Property and Casualty insurance agent for life insurance. Believe it or not, it is a complete different competency. The subject matter is different, the educational requirements are different, and the licensing requirements are different. The point is, you need to find a life insurance agent who works predominately in the life insurance field. Ideally, they would also have a focus on IUL policies.

These individuals are often affiliated with distribution companies whose names are not on stadiums. In the life insurance industry, it is more common than not for companies to "outsource" their sales function to entities called independent marketing organizations that market and sell the life insurance company's products. Many times, these companies will specialize in particular products such as IUL. With that in mind, understand that just because you haven't seen a commercial on TV for your agent's company, doesn't mean he or she should be avoided. In fact, one could make some great arguments that those are exactly the people you want to find. It is very important, however, that no matter which agent you work with, they have the ability to represent several different life insurance companies so they can use the best product for your specific needs.

While competency is obviously important, I contest that it is more important to work with someone who you feel comfortable with and consider trustworthy. In fact, studies suggest that the number one reason consumers don't buy life insurance is because they don't trust agents or life insurance companies.

38% of consumers say that they do not purchase life insurance because they don't trust life insurance companies and/or agents. (LIMRA 2016)

Now, you may be thinking to yourself, "I don't trust advisors because they are trying to sell me something." Let me assure you that you are correct, in two ways. First, they ARE trying to sell you something. There should be no mistake or misunderstanding about that fact. Selling you something is how they make their living and how they pay their bills. No different than any other profession. The question really is not whether they are trying to sell you something, but rather do you need what they are selling and is it suitable for your situation? This brings us to the second way you are correct. If your inner voice is telling you that the agent is trying to sell you something without considering your needs and objectives, then you should probably not trust them. There are a couple of red flags to look for in this situation.

The first is fairly simple. If they are talking to you more than listening, then your radar should go up. A good agent will listen to you more than talk himself to make sure he is understanding your goals and needs. The agent should also complete a Needs Analysis with you by collecting basic financial information from you. They shouldn't need your Social Security or account numbers at this point but rather get an idea of your assets, income, insurance coverage, family members, etc.

Last, you need to like the person. If you are getting a "jerk alert" then simply show them the door. Your family dreams and financial future are much too important to work with someone you don't like.

This likability factor leads us to the next point, professionals work for YOU, you don't work for the professionals. People often make the mistake of being intimidated by their doctor, lawyer or financial advisor. This should not be the case. Remember: this is your family's dreams, and you are paying professionals for their services just as you do your mechanic or lawn guy. Ask questions and raise concerns when you have them. If the professional does not respond to your satisfaction, it is quite alright to fire them and find another one who does. As they say, it's business not personal.

However, if your advisor does a great job for you and you like him or her a lot, the best way you can show your appreciation is to refer other people who may need help (and most do). Finding good clients is by far the toughest part of the job for any advisor.

One last point: I believe that your comfort level with someone can be more important than the experience level of the individual so long as the agent has professionals in his or her organization who does have a lot of experience. So, if you are working with someone who is new to the industry or specializes in another area (e.g., investments), it is quite alright to have that person act as the quarterback and bring in a specialist to help with your issues.

4. Create a Financial Strategy

Now that we have defined our dreams, created our budget to identify our current situation, and found a trusted advisor, it is time to develop our financial strategy. The first part of this process will be a "gap analysis" which will identify what you need to do to get from where you are (your current situation identified by your budget) to where you want to go (your SMART goals). Your financial advisor should have software to help you with the analysis, which is typically complimentary depending on the scope of your needs.

Once this analysis is completed, you should have a clear picture of what you need to do to achieve your goals. Warning: nine times out of 10, I can tell you exactly what the results will be without knowing you personally or your situation. More than likely, the analysis will indicate that you will need to save more money. And often, it will be a lot more money! Enough to make you throw your hands up in the air and just not try because you don't see how it will be possible. But don't panic!

It is very normal for your dreams to exceed your resources. Don't throw out the baby with the bathwater, as they say, and give up on all your dreams. Rather, you will need to go through an iterative process in which you evaluate three factors. These factors include prioritizing your dreams, evaluating your expenses and considering additional income opportunities.

I don't want you to give up on your dreams no matter how grandiose they are, but you do need to prioritize them. For instance, paying for your daughter's wedding may be more important to you than taking a trip to Antarctica. This is a tough exercise, but one that must be done. You should list your goals in numeric order but understand that your dreams are not set in stone. I encourage you to formally review

them annually and update them as needed once some goals are accomplished or circumstances change. You will also find as you go through different stages in life that priorities change. What you value now may be of no interest to you 15 years from now.

Next, you will need to analyze your budget. We all have things we spend money on that we really don't need or is just wasteful. This is where you need to make adult decisions and make some sacrifices for your goals. You don't necessarily need to eliminate the expense altogether but at least cut back. For instance, instead of your daily visit Starbucks, limit it to once or twice a week.

While most people and planners focus on reducing spending to increase savings, they often fail to consider another glaring variable. Your savings are not only a function of expense but equally a function of your income. You always have the opportunity to make more income, not just cut expenses. You can find a new job that pays more, get a part-time job in addition to your current job, or begin a side hustle (business). In today's modern world, there are all kinds of ways to supplement your income. Yes, I know you would rather be at the beach or playing golf, but the reality is that you participate in those activities at the expense of your dreams. A good idea is to find an income source from something you enjoy doing. For instance, if you are a baseball fan, consider becoming a paid umpire or working as an usher at the ballpark. If you are into financial concepts, consider becoming an agent yourself.

Once you have developed a balance between your dreams, budget and income, it is time to take action. The first step is to make sure you have your "three-legged stool" established. The three-legged stool represents the first three elements one should have in his or her plan. It includes life insurance, a will and an emergency fund. The order in which you implement these financial tools will depend on your life situation at the time. If you are a young, single person, an emergency fund should take precedence over the others and should be the first thing you establish. However, if you are married and have a family, then life insurance should be first on your list as a premature death could devastate your family. It should be noted that if you are the single, you shouldn't ignore life insurance. You should consider it if you believe you will have a family in the future as you may not be eligible in the future due to health reasons. Not to mention that the younger you are, the better the rates.

Just as you work with a professional for your financial advice, you will need to work with an attorney for your will or trust. You should also consider a healthcare surrogate, living will and power of attorney. These issues are outside the scope of this book, so I will not elaborate on them but will say your needs will vary by state, and there are some good virtual resources available if your needs are very straightforward and simple.

If we think about our financial foundation, it becomes clear that IUL can serve as a tremendous tool. Obviously, it meets the need for life insurance but is also the perfect place for an emergency fund if the policy is structured properly. Think about it. You want to make sure an emergency fund is safe. You don't want it to lose money but would prefer to gain interest rather than have it waste away in a low or non-interest bank account. You want it to be accessible but not have to pay taxes or a penalty on it if needed. By using an IUL for your emergency fund, you can gain market-linked interest with no fear of the market going down, take it out whenever you want, for whatever you want, pay zero in taxes, and have no penalty for being under 59 ½ years of age.

Additionally, although it is by no means a substitute for a will, the death benefit does go directly to your chosen beneficiary, bypasses probate, and is paid rather quickly once a claim is made.

IUL it is not a product that is going to solve all your financial needs but as you can see, it is an extremely good tool that can be used as a strong financial foundation for many.

Determine Coverage Amount Needed

When considering life insurance coverage, it is very important to make sure you have enough coverage. Your advisor will be able to help you with this calculation based on your needs and goals, but this calculation is as much of an art as it is a formula. As a result, you should not be surprised to see a large variance in suggested coverage amounts from agent to agent. You also shouldn't be surprised to find out the amount of coverage you need may be considerably higher that the number you have in your head. Sometimes, clients are surprised to see a recommendation of $1,000,000 or more, but if you consider all the future financial needs of your family, you can quickly calculate that $1,000,000 is much less than you would initially think when you add up college tuition, mortgage payments, debt obligations, retirement and everyday living expenses.

That being said, you don't want to pay for more than you need. And, unfortunately, there are some agents who will try to use an exorbitant number for greater commission. Therefore, it is important that you understand the basis for calculations.

There are several technical methods of making this calculation, and there will be a great variance based on which one you use. Among other variables, the calculations are based on your current financial picture, your age, years to retirement, and future needs based on your life goals.

One distinction to be aware of is whether the death benefit proceeds will be used as a capital fund to generate a stream of income to pay for needs or if the benefits will be amortized to meet the needs. Without invoking a Nerd Alert here, we simply want to know if the death benefits will be fully depleted over a period of time or will remain constant in perpetuity to generate interest, where only the interest is distributed to the beneficiary. The latter will require a much higher death benefit. For example, if you had a $500,000 death benefit and distributed it at 8% for 20 years, you would cover an income of $50,926. However, the capital required to generate that same $50,926 at 8% without touching the principle will be $636,575.

I am not a big fan of "rules of thumb" when it comes to financial matters, but I have to say that, in practice, the rule of thumb for life insurance is that you typically should have about 10 times the amount of death benefit as your income. So if your income is $60,000 per year, typically your coverage should be in the $600,000 range ($60,000 X 10). Again, this is a general rule of thumb. A true financial planner doesn't like this method, but with all the variable assumptions that are used to calculate the amount of death benefit, you should expect the number to be somewhere close to our 10-times rule of thumb.

The good news is that your financial professional should have software that will make these various calculations for you. The important point is that you understand the conceptual part of the calculation as we described and are comfortable with the amount you select.

Level vs. Increasing Death Benefit

When choosing a death benefit amount with IUL, you will have the option of choosing a level death benefit or an increasing death benefit. A level death benefit remains constant for the duration of the policy. For example, if you choose $500,000 of coverage, you will have the same $500,000 coverage 30 years later. There are two primary challenges with this option.

First, due to inflation, $500,000 30 years from now will be a lot less in real terms after inflation and may not be adequate to meet your beneficiaries' needs. The second challenge with the level premium option is that you don't get the benefit of your cash value account. Remember: when you die, your beneficiaries only get the death benefit, not the cash value. For example, if you had $200,000 of accumulated cash value and a $500,000 death benefit, your beneficiary would only get the $500,000 death benefit, not $700,000 ($200,000 + $500,000).

While this seems like the insurance company is being shady with this option, they are not. The cost of insurance with this option is actually less because the insurance company does not assume as much risk. Further, this may be a better option than the increasing death benefit option if your primary objective is to accumulate cash. Since the cost of insurance is less for the level option, the cash value of your policy grows more efficiently.

The increasing death benefit option has the death benefit grow as your cash value grows. Using our last example of $200,000 in accumulated cash value and a $500,000 death benefit, your beneficiaries would receive the full $700,000 ($200,000 + $500,000) upon your death.

Typically, I find the increasing death benefit option to be the most beneficial for clients but it depends on your individual goals and circumstances.

More than 1 in 4 Americans say they do not have enough life insurance protection. This number jumps to 40% when looking at consumers making less than $50,000 per year. On top of this, about 4 in 10 people (regardless of income bracket) would like their spouses or partners to purchase some or more life insurance.

Include Non-Income Spousal Coverage

A common mistake when a family does financial planning is to ignore life insurance for a non-income spouse. Many times, people just don't realize how much a stay-at-home spouse contributes to families in terms of dollars. According to Salary.com, a stay-at-home parent works on average 94.7 hours per week for an equivalent annual salary of $112,962. There is also the emotional healing process of the surviving breadwinner that can make it difficult to function for a period of time. Often, the income-producing spouse "checks out of life" and finds himself so overwhelmed that he can't function. Sometimes, as a result, they lose their business or job and find themselves in dire financial circumstances and experience even greater emotional distress. If your family has a stay-at-home spouse, make sure to secure life Insurance for them as well. It should be noted, that if the stay-at-home spouse is younger and/or female, it might be advantageous to fund her IUL for your primary savings plan as the cash value performance may be better than the working spouse's policy due to lower typical insurance rates. Have your financial advisor provide you with an analysis to see if this makes sense for your situation.

5. Get Illustrations – AND Read Them!

An illustration is a document provided by the life insurance company that define terms, states assumptions and provide legal information on the proposed policy. It is a very important document as it "illustrates" how your policy works based on the insurance company's financial and mortality assumptions. Of interest and great importance, it will provide you a projection of your policy's projected financial performance in tabular format. Remember though, it is a hypothetical projection of results based on many assumptions but should provide great insight into how the policy works and how it may perform if assumptions are met.

Your agent should give you an illustration of the proposed policy and review it with you. In fact, the insurance company requires the agent to provide you an illustration and sign a copy of receipt. If your agent does not give you an illustration, it should be a red flag that you are not working with a professional agent.

As a forewarning, these illustrations are ugly to the vast majority of people. It is not uncommon for illustrations to have 25 or more pages. They are very technical and provide a lot of confusing information. I have seen many agents struggle to explain the contents.

Still, it is very important that you actually read the illustration and ask your agent as many questions as you need. While an illustration is not part of your contractual policy, it can be used as a legal document and is normally delivered with your policy, confirms your understanding of policy features, and provides detailed disclaimers.

Note: I did not include a sample illustration in the book because they are the intellectual property of the providing insurance company and I did not want to promote an individual company.

6. Understand What You Are Doing!

Some agents like to show how smart they are and talk to you in such a way where you get intimidated about asking questions. But don't get intimidated; you know more than you think if you read this book. A good agent understands that his or her job is to help educate you on financial issues and help you feel confident about your decisions. Due to the complicated nature of the product, the agent may need to follow up with you on some of the answers, but make sure you are satisfied with the responses.

Remember: the professionals you use ultimately work for you. They may not in a technical sense, but the reality is that you have the ability to use them or not use them. It's not personal, its business and you have to treat it as such.

7. Select a Strong Company, Including Service

Insurance companies are rated on their financial strength, operating performance, and ability to meet their financial obligations to contract (policy) holders by independent rating organizations such as Fitch, A.M. Best, and S&P Global. Although these rating companies have different scoring systems, typically an insurance company with at least an A rating will be considered "Strong" or "Superior". You want a highly rated company as the guarantees in your contract are only as good as the insurance company guarantying them. Your agent should share his recommended insurance company's brochure with you that states the company's rating. As you can imagine, if the company has a good rating, a statement to such will be readily visible and if a company has a poor rating, you may have to dig a little bit. If there is any question, you should be able to visit the insurance company's website and find it quickly.

Interestingly, lower premium rates are not necessarily an indication of a strong company. They can even be a sign of poor ratings. When an insurance company has poor ratings, it has to lower premiums and/or increase agent commission to retain market share.

When choosing an insurance company, it is also important to match your priorities with the company. For example, one company may be better for cash accumulation while another might have better living benefits.

Remember: it is important to understand that the Financial Pocketknife® is not just a term to replace the name Indexed Universal Life Insurance but that it also incorporates certain options and techniques based on each individual's objectives. With this in mind, not all companies offer all the features highlighted, and there may be no one product that offers them all. This is why it is important for you to share your individual objectives with your agent and work with professionals who can advise you accordingly.

I cannot stress how important service is with insurance companies. The hard truth is that you will probably deal with the insurance company directly more than you will your agent over the life of the policy. And, frankly, that's okay as long as the insurance company has good service.

You DO NOT want to do business with a company that is going to send you through 30 minutes of automated messages, have a call center with people who are apathetic, unknowledgeable or cannot find your policy in their system because it resides in some archaic DOS-based system from 30 years ago (yes, this happens).

You also want to make sure they have a strong website with encrypted access where you can access your policy information if desired. The website, however, should not take the place of the customer service center where you get a live person.

So how do you find out if a company has good service before you submit an application? Simple. Just call their customer service center and see what happens. Feel free to ask them a question about a policy issue if you like and just get a feel for how they handle things.

8. Submit the Application

Submitting a life insurance application is very simple these days. Many of the companies now have electronic applications where the agent will fill out your information online and submit to you via email for electronic signature. Unfortunately, some companies still require hardcopy applications. These can get messy, but the most important thing to remember is to make sure you pay attention to all the signatures that are required. When you miss a signature, the company sends the paperwork back to the agent who has to track you down, have you sign, and resubmit. Bottom line, it causes large delays. If possible, opt for electronic applications as the software has built in edits to ensure the application is filled out properly.

9. List Beneficiaries/Will

Make sure you fill out the beneficiary information in your policy application and include the beneficiaries' Social Security number and contact information. Per USA Today, there is up to $7.4 billion in unclaimed life insurance benefits. While life insurance companies get vilified for this fact by the press, they don't know if someone died unless it is reported and often can't track down beneficiaries without contact information.

If you have done formal estate planning, you will want to consult your legal advisor on how to list your beneficiaries, especially if a trust is involved or there are specific provisions in your will.

10. Underwriting

Once you have submitted your application to the insurance company, it will go through the underwriting process. "Underwriting" is the practice of analyzing the risk associated with a loss (your life), determining if the company wants to accept such risk (insure it), and calculating the monetary cost the company will charge for accepting the risk (the premium).

To do this, underwriters will review your financial, medical and other relevant data. Based on this information, the company may or may not issue you a policy or it may provide you an offer price different than what the agent originally quoted. Remember: the quote you receive from the agent is only an estimate based on generalizations of your age, gender and tobacco use. If the insurance company decides you are a higher risk than the agent quoted, they may "rate you," meaning they will offer you insurance but at a higher price. There are times that they may also give you a better price because you are a better risk than estimated.

If you are "rated," it can be disappointing, and the knee-jerk reaction is to reject the offer. However, this might not be in your best interest. Before you make any decisions, you should first discuss the reasoning with your agent. Based on the circumstances, it is possible that the agent can provide additional detail to the underwriter to adjust your premium. Even if they don't make a change for you at the issuance of your policy, there are some conditions that can be monitored and re-examined in the future (say one year).

Remember, the insurance company really does want your business. It is not a personal reflection of you, rather a business decision based on their underwriting guidelines. It is also important to understand that if you are rated by one company, chances are you will be rated by any of their competitors as well.

Another option may be to adjust the amount of death benefit of your policy to better fit your budget or add some term coverage. This should only be considered if the adjusted death benefits are sufficient to meet your insurable needs. As mentioned numerous times throughout the book, the most important use of life insurance is the actual life insurance so make sure you have the appropriate coverage.

Smokers Beware

If you are a smoker, I'm not going to beat up on you and preach how you should stop smoking. I find most are perfectly aware of the negative impacts and would choose to stop in a perfect world. From a life insurance perspective, you may be able to get coverage, but it will cost three to four times the amount of a non-smoker. I know what you are going to say though, "I will get insurance as soon as I stop smoking." In reality though, this doesn't happen. I had this situation with a client and sure enough he died without it a couple years later, leaving his family in a very bad financial situation.

My advice is to get the insurance to protect your family and have your life insurance provider re-evaluate it after you stop smoking. In many cases, insurance companies will re-underwrite your policy after a year of being smoke-free and adjust your rates if applicable. This strategy also gives you real dollar incentive and motivation to stop.

11. Prepare for Your Paramed Exam

Part of the underwriting process is having a paramedical exam (para-med). Depending on the level of coverage you are seeking and your age, insurance companies will require a blood and/or urine sample. The process is convenient in that the insurance company will send an examiner to your place of choice and take your samples. The exam is paid by the insurance company, so you don't need to worry about the cost. They will also give you a free copy of your test is you request it.

Remember, when your advisor quotes you a price, it is only an estimate and subject to change based on the underwriting of your policy. We obviously want to get the lowest price as possible as the price of the insurance will also affect the cash value growth of your policy. With this in mind, here are a few tips to help get the most favorable results for the exam.

- Only drink water the day of the exam and avoid coffee and alcohol.
- Fast for 12 hours.
- Don't exercise the day of the exam.
- Make sure the sample you give is not your first pee of the day.
- If you are not a smoker, stay away from tobacco products for 24 hours prior. Avoid the occasional cigar.
- Answer all questions honestly, but you don't need to volunteer information that is not asked. Just because you have some type of medical issue, it doesn't mean the company won't underwrite your policy (insure you). Chances are they will find out through other sources including the Medical Information Bureau. In my experience, companies will work with you as much as they can, but if they feel you have been dishonest with them, they will simply deny coverage and avoid the risk. It should be noted that even if you get away with being dishonest with a company, there is a chance it could challenge a death claim based on fraud.

In some cases, companies have an automated underwriting process where they will not require a paramedical exam. Your agent should be able to provide feedback on these scenarios for you.

12. Make Sure You Receive the Policy

After you have been approved for your policy, make sure that you receive the actual hardcopy of the policy, keep in a safe place, and your beneficiaries are notified that you have the policy and where it is located. While some companies are trying to implement electronic delivery, hardcopy is still the norm. Delivering the policy is your agent's responsibility. The policy is normally sent by the insurance company directly to your agent, and he or she will deliver your policy to you and have you sign a delivery receipt. Without this receipt, your policy can be cancelled by the insurance company.

At the time of delivery, you agent should also review the features of the policy with you and make sure the coverage is correct based on your application. Your policy is a legal and binding contract which is not only needed for reference but will also facilitate the claim-paying process if needed.

It should also be noted that most states require a "Free Look" period for life insurance policies once delivered in which you have the option to review the policy's legal language and supporting materials. If, for any reason during the free look period, you decide you don't want the policy and want a refund, you can cancel it and get your money back.

13. Monitor and Adjust as Needed

Once you have your policy, you will want to review it on a regular basis to ensure that it continues to meet your needs. Ideally, your agent will contact you on an annual basis and help you with this task. If you have new life events occur such as the birth of a child, marriage, divorce, or a new home, you will definitely want to review your policy and make changes as needed.

14. Fill the Holes that IUL Does Not

As we have discussed, there are very significant Dream Killers that IUL does not combat. While several of the holes are Personal (Q4) risks and can only be mitigated by your own personal development, several of these risks can be managed through other financial tools.

First and foremost, you must have health insurance. I know this subject is messy, complicated and expensive, but the risk of not having it can ruin you and your family. A Harvard University study showed that 62% of personal bankruptcies were due to medical expenses. I have had multiple family members need surgeries that cost more than $250,000. Even events you would never think of can be devastating. A little boy in my Florida community was bit by a poisonous snake, and the cost of the antivenom serum was reported to be $198,000. While the living benefits feature of IUL can provide significant assistance in some cases of critical and chronic illness, there are too many medical issues that can only be managed by health insurance. It should be self-evident how medical challenges can be Dream Killers without health insurance.

Refer to the *Dream Killer Risk Quadrants* in Chapter 9, *Checklist Checkmate,* for additional holes and review with your financial and legal advisors. Of note, Disability risk should have a large focus as you are, surprisingly, much more likely to become disabled than to die prematurely.

Chapter 13
The Big Secret!

Inaction breeds doubt and fear. Action breeds confidence and courage. If you want to conquer fear, do not sit home and think about it. Go out and get busy.

Dale Carnegie

The objective of this book was to help you enhance your quality of life and increase your chances of achieving your individual dreams by introducing you to important financial concepts that are imperative to your success and explain in very simple terms a powerful product that may help you manage your financial needs. My hope is that I accomplished this in the previous chapters, but to be truly successful in personal finance (and life in general) there is a secret.

You often hear marketers promote the idea of life-changing products. Products that are so great that you will become smarter, prettier, healthier, wealthier, sexier and live the dream! These products, we are told, are comprised of the newest scientific discoveries or have been great secrets known only by the successful.

While modern technology and science certainly have improved our lives dramatically, the truth is that most people still fail to achieve their dreams in life and no "product" can solve that objective. But, the problem IS solvable.

In my decades of experience in financial planning, I have met and studied many people and found, without exception, a commonality among those who thrive and those who just survive. Those who struggle from paycheck to paycheck and those who have built great wealth. Note: let's not confuse income with wealth. I have seen people who make $200,000 per year who struggle to buy groceries and those who have spent their entire life never making more than $60,000 who retire as millionaires.

Here is the secret! Those who succeed in personal finance have two common characteristics: **they make adult decisions, and they take action**.

Adult Decisions

It took me some time to learn, but I finally caught on that I simply can't help some clients and unfortunately can't invest time in trying to help them. Not because they don't have a need or because I don't have tools to help them, but because of their refusal to make adult decisions. Don't get me wrong; these are the people I want to help the most and who need the most help. But, you can't want something more for someone than they want it for themselves.

Many times, I have sat with people who had financial challenges that were very easy to identify and solve, but they just won't do what needs to be done because they are, frankly, immature. Winning the money game demands making difficult decisions, sacrifice and discipline. Yes, this can be hard at times, but that is what makes an adult different from a child.

An adult must be able to recognize that he or she needs to save for the future and protect his or her family with life insurance before he or she spends money on elaborate vacations, new cars, gourmet coffee or expensive jewelry. And, they need to be mature enough to not care about class status or how others view them.

One of my favorite books is *The Millionaire Next Door*. The authors share data they collected from a comprehensive formal study on millionaires which shatter the stereotypical image Hollywood promotes and most people believe. They conclude that the typical millionaire lives a relatively humble life. They generally don't drive Lamborghinis or live in mega mansions. Instead, they buy regular cars (many times purchased used) and make 2.5 times more income than their neighbors (hence, the book name).

I have found this to be true in my own experience as a financial planner. I can't tell you how many big houses I have visited with "renters" who make tons of money yet live paycheck to paycheck. Or how many "professionals" I see who drive a Mercedes but are hundreds of thousands of dollars in debt.

On the other end of the spectrum, I have clients who have average incomes but have become millionaires. And contrary to what may be assumed, they have been able to "travel the world" and live fuller lives than most. And, without fail, they are happier than the fake millionaires because they are not slaves to debt and a paycheck.

The one consistent undeniable truth that differentiates these groups of people is one group makes adult decisions, and the others do not. I am willing to bet that since you had enough interest in becoming financially secure and took the time to read this book, that you are the type of person who does make adult decisions. But if not, it's time to start. Otherwise, the chances of you successfully fulfilling your dreams are slim to none.

Action

I often hear from people that they can't afford to save. While I completely understand that life can be challenging and saving is easier said than done, my experience is that for most people saving is not a matter of "affordability" but rather of priority.

When people say they can't save, it's sort of like the comment you hear when someone says they don't have time for something. The truth is that the task is not a priority for them. Let's test this idea.

I want you to imagine an activity that is extremely important to you. Let's assume it's an activity inside a building. Now, visualize yourself participating in that activity. Got it? Okay, now let's visualize that you hear a big explosion. An electrical circuit blew up, created a big fire, and your building starts burning. I'm willing to bet that regardless of what you are doing, you stop it and attend to the fire because it has become a higher priority than whatever you were doing at the time.

You see there is no such thing as "not enough time." There is only a ranking of priorities. The same holds true with saving. It is a matter of priority. You have to determine whether it is a higher priority than cable TV, eating out or your daily gourmet coffee. It's easy to rationalize how much you "need" those things but saving successfully requires you to make adult decisions. You cannot afford to NOT save. It is and must be a priority.

One of the consistent problems I see as a financial planner is that people think that they have plenty of time to save but CAN'T at the moment because they HAVE to pay for the car or children, etc. The problem is that there is always an excuse, and before they know it, 30 years have passed and they only have 10 years to save for their early retirement. Unfortunately, the math does not work that way; they can't save enough to meet their goals, and they are forced to live on less or continue to work much longer.

They also get in the mindset that if they don't save "this year," they are only missing out on whatever they were going to save. The challenge with this is that you can't look at that amount today, you have to consider what amount that would be in 30 years when you need to withdraw the money. Einstein stated that the most powerful thing in the universe in compound interest. Let's look at an example of that power!

🧟 **Nerd Alert! … But Read Anyway. It's Worth It!!**

Assume that we have twin brothers, Brother "A" and Brother "B." Brother A begins saving $2,400 per year but only saves for 10 years. Brother B, however, procrastinates for 10 years but then saves $2,400 per year for the next 20 years. I'm not going to ask you to do the math, but assuming they both receive the same interest rate of 8%, who would you guess is better off in 30 years?

Year	Brother A		Brother B	
1	2,400	2,592		
2	2,400	5,391		
3	2,400	8,415		
4	2,400	11,680		
5	2,400	15,206		
6	2,400	19,015		
7	2,400	23,128		
8	2,400	27,570		
9	2,400	32,368		
10	2,400	37,549		
11		40,553	2,400	2,592
12		43,797	2,400	5,391
13		47,301	2,400	8,415
14		51,085	2,400	11,680
15		55,172	2,400	15,206
16		59,586	2,400	19,015
17		64,353	2,400	23,128
18		69,501	2,400	27,570
19		75,061	2,400	32,368
20		81,066	2,400	37,549
21		87,551	2,400	43,145
22		94,555	2,400	49,189
23		102,120	2,400	55,716
24		110,289	2,400	62,765
25		119,112	2,400	70,378
26		128,641	2,400	78,601
27		138,933	2,400	87,481
28		150,047	2,400	97,071
29		162,051	2,400	107,429
30		**175,015**	2,400	**118,615**
Total	24,000		48,000	

The answer is Brother A! Despite the fact Brother A contributed $24,000 less than Brother B and 20 years less, Brother A accumulates much more ($175,000) than Brother B ($118,615) due to compound interest.

From this same example, we can calculate the future dollars that $2,400 becomes in 30 years and determine that when you procrastinate for just one year, you are not missing out on just $2,400 but rather $24,150 due to compound interest. That's right: $24,150! So, every $3 cup of Starbucks coffee is really costing you $30 in future dollars.

The underlying point is that it is imperative that you act and not procrastinate. It's a very simple idea. The sooner you begin to implement a plan, the more successful you are likely to become.

A Good Plan Is Great

One of the great challenges that I see with people struggling with implementing a financial plan is that they suffer from "paralysis by analysis." They get so overwhelmed with the universe of financial information, opinions and options that they procrastinate in making decisions in fear of not having a perfect plan or making a bad decision. Eventually, they get sidetracked by life and the next thing they know, years have passed, and they still haven't made any progress.

Here's the thing. There is no perfect plan, and you will make mistakes. We just have no idea, no matter how much we plan or which strategies we use, what the future holds and how it will impact our plan. A plan should not be set in stone and will require pivots on occasion based on the circumstances.

As a recovering perfectionist, one of my favorite quotes is, *"A good plan violently executed now is better than a perfect plan executed next week."* I have found in my business life that those who are most successful, jump into the deep end of the pool and begin swimming. This is not to minimize the need to plan but to embrace the need to act. At some point, you just have to go for it! You have to make up your mind that you are going to commit and adjust as needed.

Regardless of which strategy you choose, get busy! You can't afford to wait if you truly want to be successful.

Never Give Up on Your Dreams!

Dreams are important! They inspire us to do great things. They give us hope in times of our darkest despair. They motivate us to keep going when we don't think we can do anymore. And, they unite us as humans. Whatever your dreams are, I encourage you to be intentional about them and challenge you to make them big! Bigger than you ever thought, and don't let the world deter you. If you have people in your life who don't support your dreams, find new people! We are each capable of achieving our dreams, but it takes sacrifice. It takes hard work. It takes a resolute affirmation that you won't stop no matter the struggle.

My hope is that if you gained nothing else from this book, that you got inspired to act on your dreams and made a realization that you are responsible for them. As I have said from the beginning, the Financial Pocketknife® is not for everyone. One of my main goals in writing this book, however, was to at least enlighten people to understand what it is and how it may be able to help them with their goals and life dreams.

After all, what kind of life would it be if we didn't have dreams?

The Challenge

Now that you understand the power of the Financial Pocketknife, I want to reflect back to my previous statement in the introduction of the book. You may recall the passage:

*"The Financial Pocketknife® is not suitable for everyone.... **but let me state unequivocally, 100%, without a doubt, it is one of the most powerful financial tools ever designed to help families build a strong financial foundation.** If you don't believe me, I have a challenge for you at the end of the book that you can use to disprove my statement."* (Don't ruin it by going there now.)

So, to test the statement, I double-dog dare you to go into your local bank or traditional brokerage house and have this conversation:

"I would like you to show me a financial instrument that provides a hedge against inflation, 100% guarantees that I will not lose my money, has tax free growth and distributions, the ability to take an interest free loan, avoids probate, provides creditor protection, guarantees my family that my income will be replaced should I die, helps me protect myself financially against chronic, critical and terminal illness, and of course, allows me to take money out anytime for any reason, at any age without a tax penalty. Oh, and by the way … I only have $200 to invest per month."

Chances are, they won't even talk to you if you don't have a substantial amount of money. Some brokerage firms are known to send you to a call center unless you have a minimum of $250,000 to invest.

But if you are brave enough to accept this challenge, I would love to hear the reactions you get, so please send them to us at info@thefinancialpocketknife.com.

Questions and Answers

1. If Indexed Universal Life is so great, why haven't I heard of it before?

It is surprising how the vast majority of Americans have not heard of Indexed Universal Life. We believe there are several reasons for this phenomenon. First, the traditional life insurance distribution model incentivizes agents to focus on the affluent market and very often ignores the vast middle-class market. Second, due to its many features, IUL can be a challenging product to understand and for agents to educate their clients. As a result, many agents have not been exposed to IUL and only focus on simple products (term) that are easier to explain. Last, many in the general public find financial issues stressful and boring. They don't want to take the time to learn about "life insurance" and often avoid the subject altogether. Our goal is to help overcome all these challenges via mass communication, simplicity and convenience.

2. How much do I have to pay each month?

The amount you pay each month depends on many factors including your age, health, gender, savings goals and coverage needs. A great feature about IUL is that you can choose, within a certain range, how much you would like to contribute and can vary your payments based on individual circumstances.

3. Can I buy IUL online?

With few exceptions (if any), no. Most all insurance companies require you to work with a qualified agent to submit an application. Considering the many options that you may have, we believe using a qualified agent is in the consumer's best interest, and it doesn't change the expense structure in any way.

4. Which insurance companies offer Indexed Universal Life?

Many of today's life insurance companies offer IUL. However, not all products have the same features, options and designs. Unlike term insurance which has become "commoditized," IUL varies greatly from company to company. Further, when choosing a company, it is extremely important that you select a highly rated company as your policy guarantees are backed by the company, not the government.

5. Can I lose money with Indexed Universal Life?

Yes. While the dollars you contribute to your savings accounts are guaranteed by the insurance company not to have negative returns, there are expenses and fees that can factor into your results including the cost of insurance. Further, if you let your policy lapse or cancel it prior to its surrender charge period, you could be subject to surrender charges and/or have negative tax consequences. Read your illustration and contract in detail and seek professional guidance as needed for tax and legal advice.

6. How do I get money out of this product?

Considering you have funded your policy properly and have cash value available, you can access your money in two primary ways: a withdrawal or a loan. It is very important that you read and understand the details of these methods based on your individual policy and issuing insurance company as some restrict access to cash, especially in the earlier years of a policy. Additionally, you need to be aware that withdrawals may have tax consequences.

7. Can I transfer money from other accounts into this product?

It depends on what type of account the money comes from. You can always make lump-sum contributions into your account from non-tax sheltered accounts, such as your bank savings account. You can also transfer money from other life insurance accounts and some annuities. You cannot transfer money from traditional retirement accounts such as 401(k)s, 403(b)s or IRAs. Consult your agent and/or tax professional for guidance.

8. What if I already have life insurance?

If you already have life insurance, you can still consider IUL. You should discuss how your current life insurance compares to an IUL policy. In some cases, you may be able to convert or transfer a current policy into a new policy. It is very important you understand that it may not be in your best interest to cancel your current policy as there may be charges and other negative consequences. Under no circumstances should you allow your policy to lapse before you are issued a new policy. Consult your agent for an analysis and details on your options.

9. **Should I stop contributing to my 401(k) at work and use this plan instead?**
While individual circumstances vary, in general we do not recommend that you stop contributing to your 401(k) plan so long as you receive matching contributions from your employer. While we believe a strong case can be made that the taxation of Indexed Universal Life insurance is more advantageous than a 401(k) and other traditional retirement plans, if you are receiving a matching contribution to your plan AND expect to be vested, then it is typically more advantageous to contribute to your plan and receive the company match. However, any amount contributed over the matching amount can certainly be considered for allocation to an IUL based on your goals. Only under rare circumstances do we believe assets should be liquidated from a 401(k) and placed into an IUL, due to tax consequences. You should seek guidance from a tax professional on these decisions.

10. **Isn't the purpose of this book just to get me to buy life insurance?**
No and yes! Not to sound too much like a politician, but the answer really depends on what one infers by the question. If you are asking if the book was written solely as a tool for financial advisors to sell you a life insurance policy, the answer is "no." As evidenced throughout the book, I have been very transparent about the negative attributes (e.g., liquidity, expenses) of IUL and have repeatedly stated that it is not an appropriate product for everyone.

The purpose of this book is to educate the public on Indexed Universal Life Insurance and demonstrate how it may benefit individuals and families in achieving their life goals. It is up to you and your advisors to determine if it is appropriate for you based on your individual goals and situation.

If you are asking if this book was written to promote the benefit of life insurance as a financial tool, the answer is a resounding "Yes"! As studies show, the public is in tremendous need of life insurance and owning it can literally be a life-changing event, not only for your direct descendants but for their descendants as well. That may sound "hokey" to some, but when you personally witness a family who has experienced the death of a breadwinner without life insurance, you quickly and unapologetically become a strong believer!

Appendix – Dream Planner

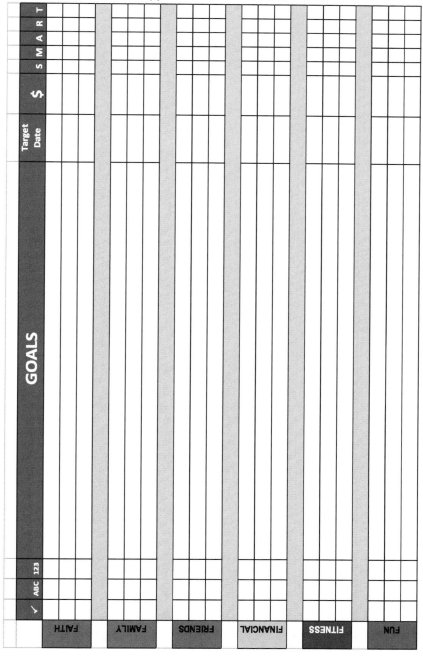